SCRAPING PEGS

The Truth About Motorcycles

Michael Stewart

Beaten Stick Press

ISBN 978-1-7774436-1-0

CONTENTS

QUOTES

"The Road to Motorcycle Joy starts around the next bend."

MARTA, Volunteer

"It is a truth universally acknowledged, that a person in possession of a good fortune, must be in want of a motorcycle."

BOB, Motorcycle Friend

INTRODUCTION
The Truth About Motorcycles

MOTORCYCLE FRIENDS

I can't get Bob's death off my mind. It puzzles me. I hate conundrums. What the hell happened to Bob?

The official cause of death? Drowning. Bob's bike flew into the Thompson River. It would make some sense if Bob was racing his Ducati, but the cruiser? The cruiser never flew. It ambled. Bob loved to do both. As long as he wasn't under glass, tucked behind the comforting clunk of a car door. Sometimes he'd scuff the sole of his boot on the ground. "Touching down," he called it, with a silly grin planted on his face.

No broken bones or major physical damage —it was straightforward death-by-water. There he was, the wind all around him; but suddenly flying, an elegant soaring swan dive, with a sudden, shocking splash down into cold, swirling water, and swimming. Or, probably, "Not Swimming", or possibly "Trying to Swim", since he drowned. There is no balance of power in the physics of trying to swim in swift water wearing heavy motorcycle boots. Force leans to the Lunar Rover Moonboots at the end of your legs, winning the clawing-upwards-but-pulled-downwards battle. Not a bad way to go, though—at least he was motorcycling before he drowned. Probably experiencing lingering JOY, not terror. Way better than just drowning. Is that the truth about motorcycling? That it embraces living and makes even the dying better? Did Bob reach a state of euphoria and decide to take the next step? The ultimate test of man and machine. Typical Bob, leaving questions behind. There was more to him than met the eye, that's for sure. That's why we got along. Our voices carried away by the wind. Laughing out loud. Singing. Crying. On a motorcycle, you can say whatever you like. Bob and I never spoke much, but we said many things.

I remember, we were at Tony's deli, when I told Bob about the time I nearly drowned in a river, dragged out inches before the Valley of Death. How to explain a near-death experience? "You had to be there," I ended up saying. Did Bob take me literally? Decide to see for himself? Who knows? Not me. Our relationship wasn't deep. Bob probably thought I was being weird, talking about passing without involving a motorcycle. I don't think this explains what happened to my motorcycle friend. Bob would have sent a clue like, "Going for a swim." He enjoyed being mysterious.

We laughed at the same jokes, enjoyed each

other's company and got along fine, but never became close. Our paths predominately crossed at prearranged events. Motorcycle friends is what we were. More than acquaintances, but not good buddies, or pals, or even chums. We hit it off, then shrugged. *Too busy and too damn difficult to make an effort in real life. It's easier on Facebook.* Why did we not spend more time together? When Bob was alive, it wasn't urgent. *One of these days I'll make an effort.* I never bothered.

Now Bob's dead. No more thinking, *we should get together for coffee or something besides motorcycles*, and then, getting together with Bunny, my cat, instead. We'll stay cemented forever in history at: just biker friends. Seems a shame now that I'm stuck at Bob-less. That was one large, lost opportunity that's hit my regrets list. Just above, "Missing the Baja Trip" and below, "Not Asking Mary McGregor for a date (before her motorcycle accident)." It's not like I have a ton of friends and couldn't squeeze in one more. Like me, Bob was socially lazy, but I'm pathetically worse; he opened the door which I never stepped through. It's a wonder I have any friends at all. Let alone a wife. I was too busy watching YouTube and polishing my forks. I know, a lame excuse. I always make time for Bunny though.

Bob was an experienced, excellent rider; really knew his way around motorcycles. He was solid. Possibly not the most skilled swimmer, I guess? Don't have any idea really—as I said, we didn't know each other well. We weren't pals and we sure never went to a beach or a motel pool together. Rode by a few on our bikes, though.

The police were equally confused, but less interested in solving the conundrum than I was. "No evidence of road hazards," they reported. "Weather was fine and there were no skid marks." *Did Bob do something stupid? Swerve to avoid a squirrel? Experience mechanical failure?* He was anal about his machines—did it turn against him in a Terminator-like twist? Or did... he... do something stupid?

The last time I saw Bob, I was the unwell one, lying in a bed at Royal Jubilee Hospital. My body was in for repair following a serious motorcycle accident. He visited; it was kind of a motorcycle event. "Wanted to get out for a ride," he said, as if the hospital was on his route.

Bob's drop-by made me think, *when I'm able, I won't let things slip. I'll put more effort into life and friendships. Starting with Bob.* Hospital patients know: life changes in the blink of an eye. Get off your ass! Get on with it. Buy a new motorcycle! Absorb the rhythm of the Road to Joy. Don't put it off.

"What type of screws do they use?" Bob wanted to know, referring to the orthopedic screws in the metal rods in my leg. "Philips or Robertson? Allen bolts?" I remember him guessing. "Stainless steel, I suppose?"

"Titanium, I think." I promised to check with

the doctor. In hindsight, screws didn't strike me as something a suicidal person would raise; then again, my mind was in Blobland when he came by. Trauma and powerful drugs will do that to you—I could easily have missed important clues. Could have ignored a pink gorilla climbing the wall next to me for that matter. Or a slimy box jellyfish.

He had brought Kirkland Almonds with him in a sandwich bag, ranting that Costco had raised their price: "Jacked them up by ninety-five cents!" Almonds weren't top of my mind then—they couldn't reach the top of my mind because they can't fly and I was exploring the inner regions of the Outer Limits. To appear engaged, I asked, "Ever think about switching to walnuts, Bob? Fewer calories and more protein." Nope, Bob was a committed almond man. And not just any almonds, Kirkland Almonds. My nut knowledge seemed to fall flat so I added, "But almonds taste way better." I appreciated Bob taking the time to put nuts in a sandwich bag for me, especially given the price increase. The cost of almonds was at most troubling. Certainly not deadly. I know Bob was close to doing a deal on a bike. Even the Costco price hike would not deny him his brand-new machine. He had fallen down an almond rat hole, but I know he wasn't cheap. He especially enjoyed spending money on motorcycles.

Suicide rumors persist, driven by the need for an answer and Bob's placid demeanor. The police questioned me about his state of mind. It's false innuendo, I'm certain. "Ridiculous speculation. Bob was not that kind of guy." Or was he? Did I mention we weren't like brothers?

I always wanted to ask him if he knew the truth about motorcycling—whether he had gleaned a kernel of insight from his years of riding. The JOY and the drudgery we chatted about. But I hesitated. Never spit it out, as they say. Afraid Bob would hear an inappropriate question, given we weren't friends who shared secrets and inner thoughts. In the absence of Bob, and with no inkling about what happened to my could-have-been friend, I turned like billions of other mortals, to the Oracle of Google and in supplication asked, "O Mighty One—what then IS the truth about motorcycles?" Having an off day, the Oracle replied, "Motorcycling is a society of rebels who refuse to live by mainstream laws and norms."

That's like saying, "Bob drowned." Cheap rhetoric. *Refuse to live by mainstream laws?* That's half the damn world now—outlaw bikers, once the undisputed kings, have slipped down so far that financial advisers and animal trainers (among others) have usurped them. Veterinarians and florists ride Harleys and Triumphs. Are they refusing to live by mainstream laws and norms? The truth about motorcycles cannot be found in popular culture. Bob likely knew but his thoughts were washed away. I waited too long to ask my could-have-been friend. I must look elsewhere.

ZEN AND THE ART OF MOTORCYCLE MAINTENANCE

Following the failure of The Sentient of Mountain View, California, to illuminate my darkness, I turned back to a book that had left an impression on me years ago when I was susceptible: Zen and the Art of Motorcycle Maintenance. Back then, I filed it under "Profound." That seemed an excellent place to continue the search for truth. I'm sure you'll agree. Why not take advantage of Mr. Pirsig's search for quality and the meaning of it all? To my young self, the book made me wonder, with deep phrases like Buddha lives in the circuitry of your motorcycle, whether these machines might be my pathway to finally getting real answers? Such metaphysical concepts, linking motorcycles to His Holiness, surely will bring enlightenment. Had Mr. Pirsig figured things out? Or was I more gullible than suggestible?

I read the words, and as they sank in, I torqued

bolts, checked valves, changed the oil, and in a dozen other ways, became one with my early motorcycles. In this unity of man and machine, engine vibrations spoke to me: I not only rode, I diagnosed. Arrhythmia, piston slap, pressure drops: with every sound and unexpected gyration, my bikes wordlessly conveyed their condition. I bought into the notion of the mystical relationship between man and inanimate objects. Would motorcycle maintenance illuminate my life?

No. It would not.

The book slipped behind me and was forgotten. I moved on; it stayed still. We went our separate ways. I experienced moments of JOY from riding, but never from wrenching. I came to prefer Marta's simple logic: "Sometimes motorcycles suck and sometimes they don't."

Now, thanks to Bob, motorcycles and truth are constantly on my mind. So, with great expectation, I began to re-read the best-selling "motorcycle" book of all time, eager to reconnect with the potentialities of my youth. *Get ready to transform*, I promised myself as I opened the magical book. *I'm ready, Mr. Pirsig! Enlighten me!*

It did not go well.

I turned my e-reader off at page fourteen. *Zen's* words were like choking down a rotten Brussels sprout. "Give it a chance," I said to encourage myself against quitting on page nine, but the expression, "There's no going back," is fact. My days of wonder had drained out of me. No longer Zen material, I had to accept, *Curmudgeonly Jackass-ism* is now my guiding light. It doesn't demand followers find answers in weird old books. If the solution isn't in a two-minute YouTube video, forget it. Except for the truth about motorcycles and what happened to Bob?

Rather than ponder the wonder of the philosopher's musings, my mind went numb–similar to the bored numbness that seeps up through the foot pegs on straight miles of nothingness. "Screw this," Jackass-ism reminded me. I put my reader down and switched to YouTube. YouTube has answers. And better video explanations than Google.

Decades of life changed me, long before I took up residence on the eleventh floor of Royal Jubilee hospital (my daughter works as an RN there, by the way. She's the #1 Angel of Mercy, that girl. Takes after her mother?).

Life changes your filters. The words of Pirsig's story were the same; his message immutable. No, in facing truth, I had to admit: it was I who had changed from a wide-eyed Zen Grasshopper wannabe to a mature, decrepit, curmudgeon. I'd accepted reality.

Life hardens people. Was Gandhi immune, I wonder? Was he able to remain perpetually child like? Is it possible to withstand the force of time? Does Professor Steven Hawking address this in his acclaimed book, *A Brief History of Time,* or is it too brief to examine the Gandhi-Time scrubbing away awe, question?

In my mind *Zen* was picked up by the Librarian in the "Profound," section and handed to the Janitor to toss in the bin, before refiling under "Abstruse." This is what happens to those twenty-year-old's who were once full of wonder and open to possibilities.

Turns out, what happened to me is what happens to every young adult, except maybe Mahatma Gandhi and Nelson Mandela? Or is that also a myth, like popular motorcycle culture? What is the truth about old Mr. Gandhi? I'll check YouTube.

Time happened. The clock ticked. Time passed, and in its passing laid more of the cards of life on the table; a bigger picture showed: not as poetic or as delicately pretty as it once had been, though it was less desperate, not as urgent, now only mildly insistent. Nowadays the good and the bad of motorcycling share equal weight in my mind. The mundane balanced with the mystical. "Sometimes motorcycles suck and sometimes they don't." I prefer Marta's point of view to Mr. Pirsig's. It fits well with curmudgeonly jackass-ism. Asses generally discourage deep thinking.

Bob liked to joke about the Zen book. "Buddha, come on up," he'd call, staring at the engine. "No need to hang out down there in the circuitry. And watch yourself if You're climbing up from the tranny. Don't want to be drain'in diced and sliced holy man out of my gearbox!"

Or, "How You enjoy'in the endless landscape of awareness Big Guy? See that handful of sand on the road? I call it the world."

Very funny Bob, I'd say.

"And the oil You're drenched in, I call it one hell of a mess."

Maybe there are people like Mr. Gandhi, who can hold on to statements like the ones in the Zen book, throughout their lives? They are soldiers. Strong. Steadfast, with resilient right brains. Fending off time as it scrubs away at "Profound". I accept that Mr. Pirsig's observations make about as much sense as any other explanation of inexplicable things. Though after my older self re-read those fourteen turgid pages, I still didn't have a clue about the really big questions, the kind the ancient Greek philosophers in Mr. Pirsig's book ponder with superlative ease: Aristotle nonchalantly wrestling elaborate theories as simply as Valentino Rossi guiding his Yamaha through a series of curves. Don't worry, I don't really understand Aristotle either, and in serious corners, at times I looked like an out-of-control SQUID (I'll get around to explaining SQUIDS to you in a bit). I remained spiritually disconnected from the Cosmos, but proximally connected to YouTube and my cat, Bunny.

Modern motorcycles insist I remain disconnected. Today's two-wheelers bear little similarity
to the 1966 Honda Super Hawk that Buddha resided
in. No tinkering by amateur mechanics: please... no
wave of Mr. Pirsig type, do-it-your-selfers, spiritually
bonding to their machines, nursing them until their
last breath. Not smart business. Industry prefers
the replace-not-repair philosophy. The art of motorcycle maintenance, tearing down a modern machine
at the side of the road using the manufacturer's tool-
kit, with or without Buddha's guidance, is history.
Now consumers are drawn in with lifestyle adver-
tisements to bond, profitably, with the latest model.
Safety enhancements, like ABS reassure timid shop-
pers. That's the sensible, money-making approach
reasonable business owners should follow. Zen has no
place in the boardroom. Gandhi would have made a
horrible CEO. *How about we all walk?* Give me a break!
Even Buddha rides motorcycles, Mr. Gandhi. According to Mr. Pirsig.

Back to Bob momentarily... Bob experienced
motorcycling JOY; the indescribable feeling riders
occasionally revel in, sitting on two wheels (or three),
slicing through air. A phenomenon motorcyclists
cherish. Bob's JOY ended in the Thompson River.
Mine ended on Highway 20—you're going to have to
wait for that story as well. It's important to mention
JOY. Pegs is about Truth. "Truth," says Marta, "Can be
pretty grim."

Bike sellers: relax–I'm determined to make it

back to your shop one of these days. May need my son's assistance. He's strong, kind, and level headed (how does a jackass end up with two great kids?). I'll demand a sizable discount on your latest model. I love to ride. You do sell mobility scooters, don't you? Motorcycle-to-scooter is a natural progression. "Often via a motorless wheelchair rolled out of a drug treatment center," Marta pointed out.

To be fair, *Zen and the Art of Motorcycle Maintenance* isn't really about motorcycles or maintenance. It's about philosophy, exploring the mysteries of the unknown. A pie-in-the-sky, clever book for the right side of your brain. The right grey mass is creative and full of wonder. My Left brain won't even have a quick peak. Left prefers Newton's *Mathematical Principles of Natural Philosophy*. Perhaps I should have reread Sir Isaac to discover Truth, but my mind had his book filed under "Laws" rather than, "Profound."

"Sometimes Truth isn't very Profound," according to Marta.

JOHN PRINE

I favour bare bones points-of-view these days. No beating about the bush. Leave Plato and Socrates out of the mix. Let's tell it like it is; not flaunting our amazing motorcycle adventures, awesome relationships, and do-it-ourselves maintenance as a pathway to a higher level of consciousness. Riders know that stereotypes and popular culture do not define motorcycling. Instead, cut to the chase, like singer-songwriter John Prine who offers common sense advice in many of his songs. You can find some of them on YouTube of course.

So, here's the deal with this book series: it's the John Prine of motorcycling. Rest in peace, John. *It is what it is, and it ain't what it ain't.* I can't argue with his logic. It is Truth. I like his songs; they keep me pointed in the right direction, unlike Zen and the Art of Motorcycle Maintenance, which is like political science, the "science" of theater.

If you're wanting the esoteric world, put *Scraping Pegs* aside and read Pirsig. If you're looking for a technical riding manual, or the drama of life as a bad boy or girl biker, or globe-trotting rides to far-off lands, this book isn't it. There are plenty of those books and YouTube videos available to enjoy. We're exploring the truth about motorcycles. We're trying to discover, what happened to Bob?

The reality is that crappy weather, careless drivers, sore asses, flat tires, death, and other aggravations creep into both life and riding. Despite years in the saddle, I haven't morphed into a stereotypical biker dude. I'm just a jackass, probably a lot like you. The truth is: motorcycles put me in a bed at Royal Jubilee Hospital. But I did discover JOY *on-motorcycle*. It can be elusive, but it's there. It's why we ride.

Press an experienced rider, and they'll admit to horrible days, mechanical disasters, soured relationships, and bad attitudes. "Like life, don't you think," Marta asks? Some, like my cousin Lenny, will show you their wounds. Then they'll step back and add, without a hint of irony, "The worst rides make the best stories." Motorcycling memories are always rosier in the rear-view mirror. Maybe that's the Zen of it?

In Marta's reality, "Motorcycle culture is sprinkled with pixie dust." But now riders have *Pegs*, an everyday down-to-earth, tell-it-like-it-is book, or series of books because, unlike the cosmos or Newtonian physics, motorcycling can't be straightened out in a single volume or a couple of YouTube minutes. It's far too complex. If it was straight forward, we'd understand what happened to Bob.

MOTORCYCLES

Because Pegs is non-fiction (albeit creative non-fiction), clarifications will be necessary to preserve integrity. To start, as you go through the pages, understand that the use of "motorcycling" in this book refers to the western recreational use of the machine. The millions of people using small cycles to help sustain their lives, know full well that riding a motorcycle is neither glamorous nor mystical. Marta guffaws uncontrollably at the thought of them reading Zen and the Art of Motorcycle Maintenance. Enjoy the book as a work of western absurdism if you're in that category. I hope you find JOY in your own way, on your transport bike.

Also know that *Scraping Pegs* holds no brand or style sacred. We're talking "motorcycles" not marketing hype or personal preference. Don't get your knickers in a knot because *Pegs* doesn't drone on about your favourite machine.

Motorcycles are like music, don't you think? Tastes change over time, from nursery rhymes, to country, to heavy metal, and so on. A category or two is skipped along the way, like Gregorian chants or Fat Bob custom choppers, but an evolutionary taste path exists. Who wants a lifetime of being stuck in a rut? How many drum solos can one listen to before knowing it's time to move on? No matter your two-wheel preference, you're welcome here.

Confession: I've lived through periods of motorcycle bigotry. I'm not Gandhi. Today I'm close to motorcycle agnostic (a serious accident will change your perspective on what's important). Admittedly, I'm developing a preference for a certain mobility scooter brand.

I've switched indiscriminately and, often foolishly, between many types and brands of motorcycles. Owned them all, or knew someone who owned one, or saw one driving down the street, somewhere, sometime. Possibly. I can't remember for sure. Bob might know, but he's not here.

Don't own a motorcycle? No problem—the logic within *Pegs* can be applied, with some alteration, to trout fishing or any undertaking. You must do a bit of mental juggling, but it is sortable. I've tested adaptability by applying the Rules to crossing the street in a wheelchair—worked great. Almost got run over once, but thanks to my Awareness, created by my adapted rules, I squeaked across in one piece. It'll be invaluable when I get my mobility scooter.

We ride (or cross streets) because it presents possibilities. It is what it is and it ain't what it ain't and that's okay, Mr. Pirsig. No need to ramble on in search of impossible answers. Marta suggests you should have told yourself this when you started pondering, "Get a grip."

MOTORCYCLE RIDING RULES

I follow ten Motorcycle Riding Rules (MRR). Keep them in my back pocket. They're there, even though I'm not riding at the moment. I have a revised version, adapted for use when not in the saddle. Made them up myself, gradually over time, as experience taught me her lessons. They're somewhat metaphysical, not black and white like the safety rules you learn in Parking Lot Cone School. They'll help you accept the truth about motorcycles, but you'll have to do some THINKING on your own. This isn't YouTube.

If you're good at adapting things, save money by avoiding the cost of a separate *How to Live A Perfect Life* rule book. Tons of people on YouTube have answers and are keen to sell you theirs (you only get the first rule free. After that you can purchase a subscription, pay up front, or watch lots of ads). Save time and money by applying MRR instead. No sense shelling out for stuff like, "Befriend people who want the best for you." How are you supposed to do that? How do you tell who wants to do the best for you? People don't come with product specifications and warning labels like motorcycles. Plus, what if you're socially lazy, like me? "There's a lot of bullshit on YouTube," Marta says.

It might sound like a copout, but reading the Rules alone isn't enough. That's why you won't find MRR on YouTube. To be effective, you must do some heavy lifting. Study the Rules, Think, Tailor them, and work at Embedding them. It's all up to you. *Pegs* isn't pixie dust. Buddha travelled to the Bodhi tree, by the Mahabodhi temple, to find His enlightenment. He didn't sit on His holy ass, waiting for YouTube to come along and tell Him what to do. Bandwidth was really slow in His day, and tablets were stone. You must also take a journey, make an effort. And be lucky (sorry, but it's about Truth, remember)?

If you want the condensed version, the Rules are mostly about Awareness and Ability. That's it. I'll share them with you. Hopefully they'll help you develop, or reinforce, a Motorcycle State of Mind. But it's up to you. It's not that deep. Of course, life is simply about Breathing and Eating.

God didn't turn over every rock in His list of ten commandments. By the way, one of the original commandments, is incomplete. Thou Shall Not Covet Thy Neighbour's Goods. What if your neighbour parked the **Motorcycle of Your Dreams** beside your It'll Do Bike with its flat tire and leaky fork?

Know that God does not condemn all motorcyclists
to eternal damnation and Hell. Do not covet the
glorious creature sitting on the motorcycle, but the
motorcycle itself, is what theologians call, "An ipso
facto clarification of the rule." Scholars cite Perfect
Creation to substantiate this modern-day interpret-
ation: Thou Shall Not Covet Thy Neighbour's Goods,
Except for Motorcycles, Two Thousand Years from
Now.

For many years I was lucky. Then I crashed. I'll
share that story. I don't want *Pegs* to be purely academic. To be honest, I found *Mathematical Principles
of Natural Philosophy* to be a bit dry, a little over the
top with its laws and theorems. Good for mopping
up spills, though. Its dryness could use some humanity and JOY for sure. Just because my gullibility has
eroded and I've fallen into Curmudgeonly Jackass-
ism, doesn't mean I've turned to stone, without feelings, lacking empathy, utterly devoid of spiritualism.
I live with Bunny, a cat, for Heaven's sake. Also, a dog,
Pearl. Cats and dogs often speak the Truth. I like to
run things by them. Too bad they can't ride motorcycles. I'd love to ride with both Bunny and Pearl. Especially now that I can no longer ride with Bob.

Bob owned a cat, Trident. Trident passed of
old age. Bob wouldn't have flown into the Thompson
River if Trident was alive. He loved his cat. Almost as
much as his motorcycles. Just a hunch.

You must absorb all ten Motorcycle Riding

Rules, so please stick with me through the Rules part of Pegs, even though it may be a bit of a grind or you may be a know-it-all, like me, and want to skip ahead. I promise, there will be a crash if you persist. Do doctors and engineers call it quits part way through their studies? *Good enough! I'm ready to drill into a cerebellum or re-engineer the Space Station guidance system. Hand me that duct tape and the hammer drill! Where's my certificate? And my Lunar Rover Moonboots?* No! They have what we call, "professional standards." I want you to be a motorcycle professional.

I see my friends at Beaten Stick Books inserted a link to provide information on "product news," and "availability." WTF? Yes, there will be *More Scraping Pegs.* I must complete a few repairs before finishing my story. Think of this marketing ploy as an inconsequential, blinking, idiot light and black it out with imaginary tape. Or don't—you might enjoy it.

https://beatenstickpress.wixsite.com/mysite

For Bob.
Kickstands Up!

PART 1 - THE DESERT

RULE #1, EVERYONE

O n a motorcycle, you're a duck at a carnival sideshow. Friends said to me, in those very words: "You're a sitting duck on that thing. It's just a matter of time before someone picks you off." Poor ducks, nailed down, crucified at a dumpy carnival sideshow. Powerless to educate themselves. Without protective gear, their survival totally dependent on dumb luck and poor aim. Round and round they go, hoping Deadeye Dick, (alias Dick, Double D (though he doesn't like that one so much) or Dicky to his friends) doesn't buy another ticket, step up with his sniper school gold medal pinned to his chest, and wreak carnage on the flock.

Kinda like motorcycles going around the streets. Cars and trucks targeting bikes. Remember, it's a jungle out there. Here's Motorcycle Riding Rule #1—take it to heart and you may spot Mr. Dick before he sets his crosshairs on your bike and pulls the trigger:

Rule #1: Everyone Is Trying to Kill You.

Climb on a motorcycle and you're in a war. Sure, its dramatic license until a nightmarish motorcycle accident ruins the English professor's narrative. Lawyers and psychologists love loosely written statements like Rule #1—they call them "major revenue streams."

"That *Pegs* book depressed the hell out of me, Doc. Just as I suspected for years, everyone really is trying to kill me! Finally, it's all laid out here in *Pegs*! Black and white. Solid, irrefutable proof. I'm not 'loopy' like you say. Who's the nutcase now, Doc? It's not 'all in my head.' And I've caught glimpses of that sniper character stalking me!"

"Do you ride a motorcycle?"

"Huh?"

"I repeat, do you ride a motorcycle? How about a scooter?"

"No."

"Rule #1 only applies when you're *on-motorcycle*. You're not going to die. It's all here in this twelve-pager from the Beaten Stick Books lawyers. Only motorcyclists are sitting ducks. Hope that clears things up. Pay Gladys on your way out. And book another appointment. You're still loopy."

Rule #1 is not to be used to validate *Chicken Little, the Sky is Falling,* delusions. Understand that the Motorcycle Riding Rules apply to, well, Motorcycling. Not trout fishing, practicing Ashtanga yoga, picking your nose, or any other non-motorcycle related activity. To be literally correct, #1 should read: *Only During the Time You Ride on a Motorcycle, Are You a Sitting Duck, and Therefore Everyone Will Try to Kill You.*

If you choose to adapt the Rules for use with other activities, do so with complete freedom, but be sure to make appropriate adjustments, add disclaimers and revise the name. Don't confuse the Trout Fishing Rules (TFR) you'll use at Samson's Trout Fishing and Ice Cream Emporium, with Motorcycle Riding Rules (MRR) or vice versa. For those of you keen on adaptation, TFR, Rule #1, for example, could be something like this: Everyone Will Figuratively Kill Me if I Don't Bring Home a Few Trout. This will help you concentrate on fishing rather than dicking around with your lure collection. You see how each activity has its own rule validation? Don't be afraid to adapt. *Pegs* is meant to be practical, not like the maintenance information in that *Zen* book which is pathetically useless.

Pay attention to, "Everyone." Take the case of my Auntie Minnie and her cute nephew, my cousin Lenny. He could do no wrong until, at fourteen, racing around in his shorts and flip-flops, on his friend's minibike, Len ran over Elly, Auntie's cherished poodle. The beloved pet had to be put down. One night, five years later, while coming through an intersection on a green light, an SUV making a left turn, clobbered Len's blue Yamaha 500. It ripped most of my cousin's right leg off. The driver: Auntie Minnie.

"The sun was in my eyes at that time of the evening," she swore in her police statement, which the police found credible: motorcycles are often invisible; it's common knowledge in the accident reconstruction business. They decided she was not on a vendetta against her nephew, harbouring a grudge over the death of her cherished pet. "We chalked it down to just another car-on-invisible-motorcycle incident," the investigating officer explained to his wife over dessert that night, a box of tasty jelly donuts. "Happens all the time. Motorcyclists are sitting ducks. That's the fact of the matter."

Lenny really should have been thinking, *every time I fire up my Yamaha, everyone, including Auntie Minnie, will be trying to kill me.* Might have saved his leg, though the weathered stub is a conversation piece now. Stumpy likes to show it off at family gatherings. Bounces a sponge ball off of it. Always makes me think—trained monkey. But I'm glad Stumpy has made good use of the two years he spent as a punk-ass biker. He told me, *Born to Be Wild,* was blaring on his speakers at the time of the crash. *Feel Like I'm Fixin' to Die* would have been more appropriate because Len never fully absorbed Rule #1. It's like being on the battlefield and thinking, *Come-on, no one's really going to try to kill me.*

Less conversationally brilliant is a girl I once had a crush on, sweet Mary McGregor. She was ravenously, drop-dead, glorious. Marta suspects Mary had a Wonder Woman, I'm invincible, perception of herself. No need to pay attention to #1. It's for everyone else. I'm beautiful and therefore special. She swerved to miss a distracted driver on Durance Lake Road. The rear wheel lost traction, skidded, then flipped Mary over the handlebars. Highsider, we call it. Too pretty to wear a helmet—she's brain-dead now though, the rest of her, the parts I was interested in, as a young lad, were fine for years after the accident. Not technically dead, but she may as well be.

Granted, the kid on the Grom really is dead, but only because old Dr. Farnsworth had a heart attack and blitzed him with a 4x4. Took the kid by complete surprise. He was wearing an approved helmet, but it didn't prevent brain bleed. Clearly the doctor was not intentionally trying to kill anyone. Nevertheless, Grom Kid is dead. He was a on a motorcycle and therefore was a sitting duck. Dr. Farnsworth is also dead—that heart attack was the first of a few until his name came up in the Death Lottery (more on lotteries later).

Rule #1 is foundational. On a beautiful, peaceful day, it's easy to forget.

Many of us say, "Don't need to read the stupid instructions." Don't carry your outlaw attitude over from furniture assembly to motorcycle riding. IKEA cabinets can be aggravating, but a Swede will not pop out of the box and blow your head off if you fuck it up. You can always return your mistake to the store and grab some meatballs. If you're an, I Don't Read Instructions Guy or Gal, understand DD will not park outside IKEA with his sniper rifle, unless there's a bike in the lot. When you swallow your KAFFEREP cookie and put the kickstand up, everyone will try to kill you.

Riders who choose not to develop a Motorcycle State of Mind are easily picked off. We'll call these "Blockhead Riders." We've all seen a few. Easy to spot Blockheads. Deadeye sits beside them with a claw hammer. Why waste a bullet? There's death amongst all that freedom and adventure on the open road or dirt track. Blockhead deaths featured on the evening news spotlight the certainty of Rule #1 so that others may benefit. Bikers pay attention—time to get serious about safety. A prospective recruit decides to buy a trout fishing rod, instead of the second hand two-wheel killer they had their eye on—that's a life saved. It's heartening to know one motorcycle death can prevent another death. Isn't that the theory of war? Kill to prevent others from being killed? Kill until the math works and peace descends on the land. Isn't it always about the math? Too much of this. Not enough of that. Let's have a war to divvy things up properly. More for me. Less for you. Every time you climb on a motorcycle, you're going to war and everyone will try to kill you. "Especially cagers with cell phones," Marta says.

Education is your defence against #1. I like

to compare motorcycle education with teaching myself how to stay healthy. Take nutrition classes: if you understand dietary guidelines then disease and the relentless attack of aging have a fight on their hands. Incorporate other tools, like medical science and good genes, and your defence grows stronger. Exercise! Get those muscles pumping. Eat some kale or enjoy a Brussels sprout smoothie if you're a Flemish outlier. Swimming lessons are worth the effort, right? An insurance policy to keep you afloat when the tidal rip catches you, though with a little luck, a gorgeous lifeguard will come to your rescue.

Motorcycle training is more complicated. Technical skills need honing and best practice tips such as *Ride Predictably, not like a jackass*, need remembering. This one also: *Worry more about getting killed than what you look like on your bike. Wear high-visibility gear and those boots that make you look like you just stepped off the Lunar Rover.*

It's way more than simply going to Parking Lot Cone School and nodding, *yeah I know all about the idiots behind the wheel who will try to kill me.* That's why there are another nine rules to help you be skillful and aware. Survival is a constant struggle. You must put your back into it. MRR will guide you away from death and injury, improving your odds of not getting killed, but I'm obligated to state: *there is no guarantee.* Even the star student at Parking Lot Cone School needs luck to survive. Her top marks won't help when a distracted driver triggers a chain of events that ends with her, well.... ending. Or at the very least, wishing she had bought a transit pass and stuck it out on the Number Ten bus. *So, what if it is always late and there's never a seat available? At least no one on the bus was trying to kill me.* All the knowledge in the world won't help when you're that duck, just a'sittin' and a'mindin' your own business while Dick draws a bead. Rule #8 deals with this truth: it's a question of when, not if, a rider will go down.

On the bright side, not riding is no panacea (yes, *Pegs* includes a little Brightness along with JOY and Hope). My friend Larry was a middle-aged organic broccoli-sprout-eating entrepreneur who refused to own a motorcycle. Despite the anti-motorcycle strike against him, we were firm friends. He knew more about health than I ever will, knew how not to be a sitting duck and wouldn't even get on the back of my bike, saying, "I don't want to die." Now he's as dead as Bob. Lar choked on a seaweed cracker. On a cracker, can you believe it! Even eating rolls the dice.

How about TV's Dr. Lean and Green, the nutritionist sales gal? Oh, yes, and Katarina Horvath, the fitness fanatic? Both also very dead. Neither one of them a motorcyclist. Their knowledge of fitness and nutrition didn't earn them a free pass, and you won't get one either with motorcycle training, because even educated ducks die. With ferocious frequency, Deadeye picks them off. It's his job, and he's very good at it.

Some perspective: germs, sugar, bacon, green-house gas, your partner, water, sex, and many other things are trying to kill you, not just motorcycles. The grim reality of existence is, as humans know, our existence will end. If you're an animal, not so grim; you may continue to live in blissful ignorance. Guess that's why my cat, Bunny, always seems so carefree and relaxed. Me, I have to go for a ride to clear my head.

Water hasn't killed me yet; crackers neither. Nor motorcycling. Nor boredom. My time will come; my number will be called but it won't be because of Rule #1.

❖ ❖ ❖

Like everything, motorcycling has a back door. I tripped and fell through it. Soft landing, nothing broken. Wasn't intentionally trying to be unethical or avoid regulations enacted to keep the greater good, good.

I never completed a formal riding course or wrote a meaningful licensing test. Didn't set out to side-step the system or snub whichever rule I had unknowingly violated. I'll say more about how I slipped in shortly, but know that, though I'm certainly can-

tankerous and stubborn, I am not a rebel or even
an activist for worthy causes: not even the righteous
struggle to keep Brussels sprouts out of restaurants
and on Flemish tables, where they belong. I was not
born with an innate knowledge of motorcycles. I
wasn't destined to become a Valentino Rossi. For me,
training was purely coincidental. Luckily Rule #1 was
drilled by my riding mentor from the get-go, who assumed if I had that one rule down pat, it might buy me
the time needed to develop Ability and Awareness. It
worked.

My back door was a desert in the Middle East.
Quite a few Double D's lurking in the shadows. Scary
looking; when you're young, folks decked out in
unconventional dress, speaking a strange language,
often glaring, are menacing, until you learn, most are
not.

Deserts appear to be bleak, no-man's lands,
when you drive by, sealed inside a car. On foot, atop
a camel, or riding a dirt bike, the land is a vast,
beautiful canvass. First, I trained on hard-packed
sand on the city outskirts; soon I graduated to hard-
packed traffic in the city. Progression is swift when
you're young, fear and caution is suppressed by naivety. Out I went, into my version of Parking Lot Cone
School: chaotic, undisciplined traffic with thousands
of riders on mopeds clogging streets already stuffed
with taxis, cars, trucks, and diesel buses belching
fumes. Throw in the odd donkey, a sprinkle of camels and some rangy goats or lambs with shackled legs

(later, I might spot one of the lambs hanging in front of a house, freshly slaughtered, its blood draining into the ditch. It put me off until I began to think, kabob).

Pour in thousands of jaywalkers playing Frogger and you have a large, polluted, congested city where Rule #1 is on steroids. A less-than-perfect student driver environment, western professionals would say. There was no doubt my friend's advice was true; "Everyone will be trying to kill you!" Death was in plain sight, many of the toothless foreboding looking figures, seemed eager to execute me. Killers were everywhere, not like driving in Porto, Edinburgh, Osaka, or Omaha. I had to learn quick or die trying.

Killers are on all roads, EVERYWHERE, not just the Middle East. There's no asterisk on Rule #1, *Except as listed on the Peaceful Locations website. Dedication to mastering the killing varies from place to place, but the rule includes "everyone," for a reason. Calm and orderly can fool you. Complacency will kill you. Spaniards, Scots, Japanese, and Arabs are all trying to kill you just as much as Nebraskan farmers and the Gandhi-like Jain followers in India.

I will grant you, in the interests of fairness, that these "killers" do not have a conscious desire for your death, nor do they drive Stephen King-like "Christine" mobiles that are fueled by insatiable bloodlust rather than gasoline. No, it's much more sedate; which you can take great comfort from as you pick

your bike out of the ditch that super safe family Volvo
left you and your battered bike sprawled in, on its
way home from the Festival of Peace, Light, and Harmony. The occupants' faint conversation heard on
the breeze as it drives away:

"Oh, did anybody notice that bumping noise?"
"Think you clipped a cone, or maybe a duck
crossing the road, Mum."
"Ah, poor little thing... Are our peace and harmony souvenirs in the back okay, Son?"
"Yes, Mum, they are and hey, look: there's that
nice Mr. Dick. Showed me his gun once."

After I left the Middle East, I occasionally pro-
vided technical support to risk lawyers—that is, lawyers who specialize in risk mitigation. And just to
mitigate the risk that you have no idea what risk
mitigation is about, it's about reducing the chance of
something happening. More accurately, it should be
known as the specialization of sucking the joy out
of life. Which really sucks. We can summarize their
views as:

1. enjoying life is risky, so don't;
2. there's good money to be made advising

bureaucracies on ways to strip all enjoy-
ment out of products and services;
3. at a minimum, add a six-page warning
   preamble to all product manuals;
4. always wear expensive business attire;
5. frown a lot when the word "carefree," is
   mentioned.

We shared a few motorcycle discussions. In
fairness, the lawyers agreed everyone is trying to kill
bikers. Even showed me their handbook on safety. I
stopped reading at *Everyone, Everywhere, All the Time
is trying to Kill Everyone. Your safest bet is to buy a tank
and drive at a safe pace—walking speed is suggested, stationary is ideal. Motorcycle owners should sit on their
machines in the garage. With the engine off. By sit we
mean not on the bike, but on the floor in case the bike
falls over. Sit far enough away from the bike that if it
falls over, it won't nail you. Even in your garage, keep an
eye out for lightning, floods, snakes, loose electrical cables,
box jellyfish, zombies and/or invading aliens. Intruding
motorcyclists attempting to lure you onto your bike is the
supreme threat. Keep a shotgun handy for defence against
these monsters. By handy, we mean triple-locked in a safe
secure cabinet with appropriate paperwork.*

In other words: safe, but risk-free. "Of course,"
I couldn't help pointing out, "You can die eating a
cracker as well."

They'd shoot me their, *nobody likes a smart-ass
who doesn't take risk super seriously*, glare. I was re-

scheduled to make room for "cracker box warning label" meetings. Fine by me.

Valid as their recommendations are, the risk folks fail to see the actual point: that of Life itself. *Carpe Diem* and all that. Thank the Heavens, there will always be the subset of riders with over-blown confidence, who will twist the throttle despite the prevalence of shit-happens Volvo drivers, road hazards, Blockheads, and their own inevitable demise.

But that is what it means to be human, and that's utterly reassuring. Wet blankets muttering from the sidelines won't put an end to cornering faster than a fully loaded hay truck. The global speed standard endorsed by highway safety councils worldwide—a standard the Risk Team would love to see lowered to zero.

I say: overtake that dawdling hay truck! Don't just overtake it: hold up your motorcycle training certificate, stand on your foot pegs and proudly yell: "I have a chance. I understand Rule #1. It's real. I intend to learn all ten rules!" If you're in one of those jurisdictions that have outlawed standing due to risk, do it anyway. Fuck it! Be an outlaw! Eat a cracker. Don't bow down to the wet blankets in the risk department! You're a motorcyclist who doesn't follow society's norms. Remember Mr. Googles?

Scrape Your Damn Pegs!

Then sit down, jam that accelerator open, bear

down in the corner and lean until sparks fly. Cover your ears, my legal friends. The truth about motorcycles and life is, both are risky. But, as you say, "Fortunately, there is real good money in it."

RULE #2, YOU

A large, well-respected study found 25% of motorcycle accidents involve a single vehicle and no murderous inanimate objects. Be it Blockheads gunning down empty roads, on MV Augusta's at two in the morning or middle-aged moms and dads, enjoying their third ever ride on a peaceful Sunday afternoon. YOU can be your own worst enemy.

Rule #2: Don't Kill Yourself by Doing Something Stupid!

Yes, included in the "Everyone" of Rule #1 is... you. It's not just Auntie Minnie and Dr. Farnsworth stirring the pot, or OTHERS who are to blame, it's YOU. Be Accountable! Much of the time it's STUPID YOU! 'Stupid' is a pervasive human trait and as the saying goes: *You can't fix stupid.* Well, maybe yes, maybe not, but at the very least Rule #2 will help you RECOGNIZE stupid behavior, which may at least save your ass.

Everyone can be STUPID, even Mr. Gandhi. *I prefer to always walk, never to ride*—stupid! Ask Mr. Google or Mr. Pirsig; it's well known that *on-motorcycle* is the path to enlightenment or at least, uncaged free-floating thought. Or death, if you're a Blockhead.

My risk lawyering friends add their safety preambles to product manuals in an attempt to prevent stupid, but we're all too weak in the head to read them. Just kidding! The warnings are there to defend clients against litigation. No one cares if you actually read them or not, as long as you check the little box that says you did. MRR doesn't have a preamble or a *Read and Agree* box. You consent to put your life on the line when you climb on.

You're thinking Rule #2 is obvious. That it's common sense and shouldn't be a rule. It's nonsensical how uncommon common sense is, isn't it? Especially when you're young and driving a V-Rod.

What's obvious to you might not be to me. Back to the story of falling through a back door. I didn't get all the facts quickly. I was what they call a "slow learner," with the Motorcycle Riding Rules coming to me over many years. I went to the School of Fly by the Seat of Your Pants, instead of Parking Lot Cone School. All smart people start off STUPID. To learn the rules, I had to roll up my sleeves, use my own noggin, and keep my wheels on the pavement for years; not like that other guy who also got a set of ten rules. We're told he went up Mount Sinai—what we're not told is that he undoubtably rode a dirt bike. God didn't want to hang around while Moses struggled up the mountain in ratty, homemade sandals. That would be STUPID! Why linger when He knows about dirt bikes? At the top, boom went the lightning strike. One-minute humanity is rudderless, the next, Ten Commandments! On the original tablet, with a 1 foot by 2-foot screen—one for him, one for Sarah, so there was no arguing over who would watch what and when. I wasn't there, but I'm sure God also gave Moses saddlebags to bring the tablets down the mountain on the holy dirt bike in a safe manner. "Don't be STUPID, Moses. Use the saddlebags." No Lunar Rover Moonboots to replace his crappy sandals, though. "Careful on your way down, Moses," God said. "Everyone will try to kill you." Kidding – that was Marta being a Smart Alec.

Moses received the Rules for The Entire World; I made up my rules for myself and the few who care to read them. I wrote on a note pad I stuffed in my tank bag, then laboriously typed them into my tablet.

I practice Curmudgeonly Jackass-ism; we're not a deeply religious bunch. However, I have a hallowed belief that my first motorcycle, a Suzuki TS-125, was a direct descendent of the Moses Mount Sinai dirt bike. An altar to remember a holy event. It'll be revealed when they stumble on The Motorcycle Testament. Moses and I share the feeling of standing on pegs, feathering the throttle, defying gravity as it tries to pull us down, but rising. Up to where God is. The Father of Motorcycles.

It's worth considering the fact that, had life been encumbered by risk management in the year 1300 BC, Moses would have kept God waiting while the Holy Lands Risk Department debated the dangers of ascending Mount Sinai. Then another long delay while each Commandment got a minimum six-page cautionary warning preamble and God disclaimer. Come to think of it, religion has its own Rule #1: Every Mainstream Religion is Trying to Kill Every Other Mainstream Religion. Maybe not? I don't know. Did I mention I'm not deeply religious? But from watching TV news, it sure seems like it could be a rule?

God's rule, "Thou Shall Not Kill", is explicit. It means "Do Not Kill Dead." D.E.A.D. Finito! For both MRR Rule #1 and Rule #2, "Kill" is more generic, a cover-all term, not limited to its use in Deadeye's sniper training material, or on ancient slabs of stone commandments. In MRR, we extend kill to include injured. Dead to include maimed, paralyzed, coma-tose, castrated, disfigured, impaired by PTSD, or any other condition that will have you thinking, on a bad day, "Good day to be dead."

If it's PTSD you end up with after your motor-cycle crash, the cool thing is: you may get a free service dog. Won't be a top dog, like my Pearl, but probably a good listener like my cat, Bunny. My brain-dead ex-dream girlfriend: Helmetless Mary,

didn't even get a goldfish. Experts say some coma-
tose people can sense their surroundings. When I'm
capable, I'm going to pop over and leave Mary a fish.
I hope the care centre risk folks won't object. Maybe
two goldfish—she deserves it. Plus, I'm curious—did
even a speck of ravenously drop-dead glorious survive?

◆ ◆ ◆

Recent safety school graduates have the benefit of studying a comprehensive formal curriculum
compiled by experts, but many prefer instead to
watch, *how-to pop a wheelie* videos on their phones.
Surely, they have all the knowledge they need when
they venture out onto their first road or trail?

News reports suggest some don't. They gradu-
ate and in less than no time do something monumen-
tally STUPID, sometimes into a monument. Blockheads! They have absolutely no respect for Rule #2.
What was Jock Crotchrocket Jones-DeSilva, today's
casualty on the local news broadcast, doing during the lesson on "How not to kill yourself?" Doodling sport bike sketches and FaceTiming his parents
whose latest news was the emission-free gray tank in
the garage they purchased, taking advantage of the

government grant political scientists ratified at their convention in Bali.

With one more body added to the "splattered over public infrastructure" statistic, Crotchrocket may well have wished he'd removed the Brussels sprouts from his ears and paid more attention in Safety Class; though we'll never know, God rest his soul because he did something STUPID.

Thankfully, he was the only one splattered across the road and off his short lived, outlaw racer persona, so all's well... that ends with only the one to blame in the morgue. But alarmingly, they're often NOT the only injured. And that's just downright annoying. Motorcyclists often take others down with them.

After all I said, you might still think that Rule #2 is common sense and could be rolled invisibly into Rule #1 or dropped altogether. *There's no need for such esoteric nuances. We're talking throaty motorcycles, not splitting hairs*. I'm an expert rider and never do anything STUPID. You may well be right, so I'll tell you what we'll do: we'll remove Rule #2 when there are no news stories of preventable motorcycle accidents for one week. I was going to say "in the world", but I'm confident enough of its merits to limit it not just to one country, or a state. I'll just use one city—I say "city", I mean Pirsigville, population 326. Last week it was 327—heard there was a rider-at-fault crash out on Highway 27 on the weekend. Or, I'll remove the rule when Hell gets a light dusting of frost, or when Risk takes over the world (hmmm, sounds like a great idea for a board game. Wonder what to call it...) and restricts interactions with motorcycles to our garages. Whichever comes first.

Be aware: don't turn yourself into a motorcycle statistic—even you are capable of STUPID. That's two rules. You'll be expected to know ten by the end of the book (don't cheat and look at the list in Appendix A). There's no test—that's out on the road, getting killed or not. MRR isn't like forcing a Newtonian to learn medieval Albanian poetry, Ability and Awareness have practical value. It's up to you; I'm not going to get killed because you weren't thinking when you took your eyes off the road. I'll be watching for you, driving my mobility scooter, so please be careful and don't slam into me. Please tell me you remember both rules. Great; let's move on and learn Rule #3. It's very dry, but essential to not killing yourself on a motorcycle. Sorry, there's no cutting corners. Remember the last time you did that? Came close to being splattered on a long-haul semi with a skull and crossbones decal on its hood. STUPID.

RULE #3, PHYSICS

Steven Hawking wrote the acclaimed academic book, A Brief History of Time. It's astrophysics, or, "Physics sprinkled with pixie dust," as Marta, a volunteer at MRR Labs, (aka my garage) calls it. Tony, proprietor of a local deli, has read the store's copy of Steve's book. He told me it's, "Flakier than my pastries," but then I don't think Tony knows what he's talking about. He's more of a mayonnaise guy than astrophysics expert. Rides an Indian, though (apologies to First Nations people). A nicely dressed Indian (better?). Sometimes Tony and Marta ride together. Marta has an old Guzzi. Steve was stuck in a wheelchair.

A through knowledge of condiments, is commercially of much greater value than black hole expertise, if you're operating a deli on Earth. Marta says, "I like the fact that Tony's deli, unlike astrophysics, offers battered pickles. It's a big plus." The sad truth is, if Tony wrote, A Brief History of Delis, the book would not be lauded by academia. Ditto for saving lives by sharing motorcycle rules. Academia is only interested in pixie dust. It's a sore point amongst deli owners and motorcycle authors.

Motorcycle physics deals with terrestrial forces, following the foundational work of Sir Isaac Newton. Pure science. The Laws of Motion. The Law of Inertia. For extra credit, read Sir Isaac's book, *Mathematical Principles of Natural Philosophy*. Sorry, there's no YouTube video, I'd make one if Mary McGregor was able to help present, but a motorcycle nixed that dream. Newtonian physics is nothing like the ancient Greek musings included in the *Zen* book.

Valentino Rossi didn't study abstract ideas or political "science" to learn how to get around corners safely, and neither should you. You're a motorcyclist, not ET, Uranus (the ancient Greek God), or Karl Marx.

Before we start, please ensure you have a calculator app, a picture of IBM's Watson computer, Mr. Newton's portrait, or for very old schoolers, a slide rule in sight. You won't be required to use them, but lift your gaze from the text occasionally and take in a visual reminder of the topic. It's what educators call a "training aid." The image will remain with you and help you remember Rule #3, the way a sexy pinup arouses you, like Mary in her glorious bikini days; only her image will probably have the opposite effect of contemplating physics.

In honour of Sir Isaac, MRR Labs presents the next rule:

Rule #3: IGNORING Motorcycle Physics May

Kill You

Marta made up a corollary: studying astrophysics will not help you out on the road, unless you're confronted with a pothole the size of a black hole.

My mastery of the Newtonian Laws Concerning Motorcycles was initially limited to what is achievable riding a small displacement dirt bike in the desert (although my yellow Suzuki TS-125 was relatively large and conspicuous in a city teeming with mopeds). If only Newton had lined up his apples in the sand, at regular intervals, to teach me how to brake, lean and counter-steer. Occasionally throwing fruit to test my reflexes. That man knew his stuff, apples and lean angles. Perhaps when bikes travel on Mars, Steve's book will find a spot beside *Mathematical Principles of Natural Philosophy* on the of shelves of motorcycle engineers.

Sir Isaac Newton

I had to wait until I returned home to the west coast to really absorb Rule #3. You don't do a great deal of high-speed highway driving on a TS-125, and the physics of navigating a small dirt bike up a hard pack sand hill, is pretty much instinctual, when you're young. Even Moses figured it out, and, like me, he never attended Parking Lot Cone School.

In the desert there are no corners that tighten up, in what I would learn is called a decreasing radius. Drifting wide in a desert turn is not a big deal. It won't end your life. You have two hundred miles or so of extra space to get your machine under control. Lean into the wind. Let the bike fly. No need to haul out the Laws of Motion or study the formulas you slept through in physic's class to correct your behaviour. Just drift. But no scraping pegs. Enjoy a battered pickle or two.

Fortunately, by the time I discovered tight curves on man made highways, there were YouTube videos that explained the science of motorcycle physics. What to do when the choices, depending on your direction of travel are: run wide and crash off road or ride into oncoming traffic and initiate a head-on collision? Maybe learn to sharpen up your turn by countersteering and leaning. Navigating corners on a motorcycle is much more complex than calculating the mass of an atomic atom which, as we know, every time we do the math is $1.67 \times 10\text{-}27$ kilograms, for one of the periodic elements (was it carbon or that new one, ununseptium? Doesn't matter, ask Marta if it's troubling you). Math isn't nebulous, which is why Watson is so good at it. It's always the same answer.

Put Watson on a KTM, and he's lost.

Atomic mass is predictable. Corners, though? Same answer each time? Not a chance. The question doesn't even stay the same. A corner on a motorcycle is a crap shoot; weather, road conditions, traffic, wildlife, radius, slope, and your skill level are all at play. Especially your skill level, so thank the stars you respect Rule #3. And that's only ONE corner–there's another one just down the ribbon of black twisting asphalt, and then a thousand more. A thousand potentially lethal questions. The physics always in motion, testing the rider's skills. You don't have to geek out on Newton's formulas and logic. Understanding how to apply his body of knowledge is what Rule #3 is all about; mostly how to lean, counter-steer, brake, and throttle control.

Interestingly, riding, unlike nuclear physics or oil painting, requires both left and right sides of the brain to function in tandem. Michelangelo's left brain slept through much of his gorgeous work on the Sistine Chapel. Robert Oppenheimer didn't use his right brain at all when he invented the atomic bomb. Perhaps he should have? Try not using either your left or your right brain when you're motorcycle riding and You. Will. Die. Monday mornings tend to see neither side of my brain functioning, let alone in tandem. They may start waking up by lunchtime. Left will go back to sleep by midnight. Right usually stays up a while longer. Be Brain Aware before you climb on and twist the throttle. Are both sides operational? Know that while Sir Isaac could depict motion using formulae, he was not able to ride a motorcycle. Who would have made a very skilled rider? Leonardo da Vinci. Perfect left and right brain balance.

Be skillful: study motorcycle physics. But remember, not all coconuts are designed to be placed inside a helmet. Here's a best practice Left-Right brain tip to start you off:

Counteract target fixation: look where you want to go.

◆ ◆ ◆

Away from the desert, on a good old fashion twisty two-lane western highway, before I'd fully absorbed Rule #3, I realized: I'm going to kill myself trying to keep pace with my race-track friendly riding buddies. *They understand high speed, braking, and cornering motorcycle physics. My time's been spent trying to avoid death under entirely different circumstances.* My haphazard Fly by the Seat of Your Pants schooling, had gaps that could turn deadly because I did something STUPID. I didn't confess, "Hey guys, I don't have a clue about high-speed cornering. My school was the wide-open desert. Please teach me your ways," because like most illiterate adults, my lack of formal education embarrassed me. Instead, I boned up... for safer bones. I learned on the sly and you can too. It's not difficult. Unlike riding in the desert, for highway riders, knowing the science of riding fast and surviving is crucial. As is the science of slow speed maneuvering on bikes larger than a TS-125. Ever had an 800lb / 365kg Goldwing topple over on you?

With more appreciation for the principles of inertia and momentum, I was soon scraping pegs on corners without the terrifying fear of death lurking over me, and I stopped panic-braking–a telltale sign of a Blockhead with little knowledge of Rule #3. I understood the importance of preserving space. One day I may become really proficient, but for now I'll settle for not freaking out and doing the wrong thing at the wrong time. After all, I'm not aiming to become Langford Track Champion. I just prefer not to kill myself when I'm out on a rip, twisting the throttle, saying hello to life, because I was too stupid to master Rule #3.

It was different in the old days of motorcycling. Physics wasn't as big a deal. A 1968 BSA Rocket 3, or similar age bike, and a Hayabusa or Livewire, are totally different machines. Riders back in the day didn't have to master rocket-like acceleration and ridiculously high speeds. They could get away with Rule #3: Very Lite. Technical riding skills used to be the dominion of track professionals. Today everyone's a Valentino Rossi. Don't wait till you're drifting wide into oncoming traffic to say to yourself, guess I shouldn't have ignored motorcycle physics. This YZF-R1 is a lot peppier than dad's old R50.

Thanks to clever engineering, riding skills can be tucked away in abeyance much of the time today. Riders can concentrate on traffic and road conditions while their machine guides itself through curves, corrects panic-braking and other bad habits motorcycle engineers have been able to compensate for. Modern motorcycles can bore because they often demand little of the driver. It's like spellchecker. You no longer need to spell, right? WRONG! Only if you want to come across as an illiterate Blockhead. You must have language skills tucked away ready to deploy when spellchecker trips over a "to" that should have been "too" and kicks off WWIII.

Engineers have transferred responsibilities from drivers to sensors and computer brains. Riders become complacent. But there's always a pop quiz up ahead. Our driver is on auto-drive, travelling faster than an old school track racer. The sun blinds at the apex of a tight curve. If your technical riding skills aren't honed and ready to deploy instantaneously, Deadeye will have you in his sights. Finito! *Counter-steering could have gotten you out of that nasty drift, but you never really mastered the skill. Oh well, another notch for the Dickster.*

This best practice tip will help you think about your physics education:

Devote time to learning about front end rake, trail

geometry, and camber thrust instead of loud pipe audio dynamics.

Speed reduces time. I'm not going to drone on about how that complicates Rule #3. Check out Steve's *Time* book. Tony, at the deli, will lend you the store copy if you purchase the Cosmic Special. It comes with two battered pickles.

Motorcycle education is not so much science physics class, or an elegant art lesson. It's more like painting with calculus. If you don't want to do the math, stay the hell off the highway! If you don't like art... you got it: also stay the hell off the highway. Make sure both sides of your brain are in the game. For me, that's the aforementioned noon to midnight window. Outside of that time frame, I'm titling too far toward Sir Isaac or Pablo Picasso. I should be *off motorcycle.*

Isn't it enough that everyone, including yourself, is out to kill you? Must you also ignore the laws of physics? Take Dicky D... despite his natural marksmanship, did he rest on his laurels like his brother Radical? No, he devoured the mental and technical knowledge necessary to win a boat load of marksmanship gold ribbons. "And wreck havoc at the carnival," Marta reminds. Motorcycles and guns are both dangerous. If you can't be bothered to educate yourself, take Risk Mitigation Guy's advice and hunker down. Sit in a tank, going nowhere. Or, like our carnival ducks, you can only hope that your dumb luck doesn't run out.

Leonardo da Vinci Vs Valentino Rossi. Who wins? Let Marta know.

http://www.facebook.com/beatenstickpress

RULE #4, KILLER BIKES

Have you seen the movie, Christine? About a Plymouth Fury with paranormal super-powers and an evil mind of its own? Christine is a car that goes on vendettas and kills people. For research purposes, Marta arranged a viewing in my garage, or as we call it, the Lab, along with The Car and Maximum Overdrive. Unsalted, butter-less popcorn, plus tap water provided. Lots of grumbling about the cuisine. "Next time, Brussels sprouts," Marta announced! Did I mention the Lab staff are all volunteers? A few retirees and a couple of out of work types, hoping "MRR Labs" will look good on their resumes. They're not, "in it for the money," but I haven't yet worked out what they are in it for. Still, I must encourage Marta to loosen up on the snack budget.

One retiree has white coat syndrome. Likes to dress up in the recycled lab uniforms Marta wrangled as a donation. Unlike the other volunteers, he has no interest in motorcycles. "I'm a trout fisher," he declares proudly, as if it's a superior calling. When you're not getting paid, people will only put up with so much horseshit. How do you fire an annoying, scatterbrained, trout fishing volunteer? I think I'll assign that task to Marta. She's been chomping at the bit.

Here's the logic the folks in my garage grappled with as they dislodged bits of popcorn from between their teeth:

If Buddha can live in motorcycle circuitry, as suggested in the Zen book and applauded by epistemologists, can the Devil also take up residence in electronic components?

To quote Lab findings, "The notion that the devil can be embedded in a bike, is **balderdash**. The devil-car theory lacks credibility and is a lackluster attempt at the quick buck school of marketing." The report states that the Killer Bike phenomenon originates with human error — "primarily inappropriate selection or neglect," or as Marta puts it, "Dumbasses not paying attention to Rule #2."

Other than trout fisher, the lab volunteers are all pretty clever. I don't understand why some aren't able to find jobs? Do they spend too much time riding motorcycles and watching terrible movies?

My first motorcycle was the exact opposite of a Killer Bike. I bought it five years after the publication of *Zen and the Art of Motorcycle Maintenance*. Young, curious, and restless, I was more interested in Zen itself than motorcycles. I'd putted around on friends' small bikes, mostly on dirt roads. Had some-one predicted, "One day you will own a motorcycle. It will be your sole source of transportation," I'd have answered them, "Nonsense. I'm pragmatic. A tech-nologist. Ones and zeros. Newtonian physics. Why drive an impractical toy when I can buy a car? Where would I put my stuff? Or Mary, if she agrees to go out with me? Besides, the weather can suck and I might die." I wasn't familiar with Killer Bikes at the time; there are lots of less dangerous reasons not to own a motorcycle. I agreed with all of them.

Here's how destiny got flipped around and I be-came the proud owner of a cheerful Suzuki.

At age twenty-six, I sold everything I'd accu-mulated in life to that point, which could be defined as "a bunch of mostly worthless crap," to work for an engineering company on the other side of the globe. I'm somewhat older now, yet I seem to have bought pretty much all the worthless crap back again. I'm a technologist, not an engineer which isn't great if you're working for a consulting engineering com-pany. Like Junior Nurse in an office of uppity special-ists. "Bed pan call on the design floor. Calling, Mr. Stewart!" Thank god Larry's funding came through to help make MRR Labs a reality. He left me $1,464 in his will following the death-by-cracker incident, "for your dangerous motorcycle hobby." I budgeted $732 for snacks, under Marta's control, and spent $23.16 on a Larry Memorial Plaque. Marta has added, "Budget Management," to her resume, "In case I allow myself to be hired."

Living in an apartment in large, hot, polluted, chaotic Middle East City, I made friends with another expatriate and his wife, both of whom had dual-purpose 250cc motorcycles, shipped over from Vancouver, Canada. The couple rode their bikes on hardpack desert sand, and used their Citroën 2CV, the weird French two-cylinder, air cooled, economy car for urban driving. They were too smart to ride in the city, understood Motorcycle Riding Rule #1, owned a car, and acted accordingly. They spoke about the wonders of riding. I'd heard about the wonders of sex. The wonders of travel and food, but had never witnessed the eye-sparkle of people thinking, *on-motorcycle.* Riding in any direction. Discovering ancient ruins. Old caravanserai. Eating in decaying, central courtyards where weary travellers rested hundreds of years earlier. Visiting remote villages and meeting the shy, hospitable people those ancestors have lived in the same area for centuries.

Politics, religion, colonialism, totalitarianism and other socio-economic-isms were all running rampant in that part of the world. But I won't go there. *Scraping Pegs* has its plateful, bringing the truth about motorcycles down to earth. Societal issues? That's another kettle of fish best left for a different chef. Or is it? Motorcycles can produce moments of Absolute Clarity for riders with a Motorcycle State of Mind. Perfectly balanced thought. Do riders not have an obligation to share their profound, pragmatic, uncaged brainwaves? For the Greater Good of Humanity? Political science is struggling, some suggest on the verge of going under. Surely, they would welcome a helping hand?

The year before I crashed, I rode the Pacific Coast Highway. There was a tremendous amount of political theatre in the water, in the air, and on the highway. It was inescapable and so thick it threatened to push me into despair. I rode until this moment of Absolute Clarity eased my mind and scraped my pegs:

Constitutions worldwide, must mandate leaders walk or ride motorcycles on their soil. Will you be taking Motorcycle One today, President Rider? Our leaders would get along famously if we took their limousines away and plunked them down on two wheelers. Get them out of the cages that wall them off from the people they adore and strive to serve. Isn't that what they're always going on and on about?

Place them closer to the citizenry, the group they sacrifice their personal wealth and freedom to serve. Instead of hiding behind endless reports, place them in the environment they cherish and promise to cleanup and protect. Life embraces motorcycle riders. Cruising around their dominions would connect our rulers, not wall them off, isolated in the back of chauffeur-driven armoured limousines, denigrating people sitting in the back of other armoured limousines. Sure Deadeye, or this brother, Radical Dick would pick off a few, but fresh blood is golden in the leadership game. There is never a shortage of egomaniacs prepared to step up and serve the citizenry.

Motorcycles are excellent Thinking Machines. Which profession is most in need of help with THINKING? Motorcycles lead riders to inspired answers. They screen out people whose left and right brains don't work in tandem; people incapable of operating motorcycles sure as hell shouldn't be running countries! "Or hamlets, either," Marta pointed out when I filled her in on my bright idea.

Isn't that all we want from our leaders—intelligent answers, getting along, and well-balanced brain functionality? No flipping out about left and right politics. Sure, a few outliers would sneak in, like North Korea playing the extreme hermit chopper dude, but generally, motorcycling is a welcoming community. So, let's sell the UN building, fire the chauffeurs, donate the limousines to one of those boots-on-the-ground charities run by volunteers (like MRR Labs), buy each leader a bike and a helmet and tell them not to come back until they have solid pragmatic answers and are all pals. Ride an electric bike if you're anti-fossil fuel. No excuses. No tribalism! No more theater games! Fact based reporters may tag along.   #WorldLeadersOnBikes. We'll clue them in on the Motorcycle Riding Rules and how to change their oil, before The-World-is-My-Oyster-and-We're-Going-to-Save-It, road trip takes the starter's flag.

Don't you think world leaders should know how to change their own oil? Shouldn't that come before changing the socioeconomics of a country? If you can balance a motorcycle, there's a chance you may balance your country's budget. If you stop to assist stranded riders, you'll likely give our forsaken a hand up.

What's the down side? "Motorcyclists couldn't possibly screw things up worse than our political scientists have," Marta said.

I didn't have moments of Absolute Clarity *before motorcycle*; I was plodding through life, like everyone else who doesn't ride, in a brain fog, buying junk I didn't need. Living in a room on the outskirts of Blobland. I didn't have a plan, like in the Zen book, to ride a motorcycle on secondary roads to Yellowstone, postulating along the way.

Starting me on my two-wheel path was a Suzuki TS-125 with a dual gear shift, giving it eight gears and a lot of range. I had zero motorcycle smarts (Marta says I'm lacking in several other areas as well, like budget allocation and firing dumbasses). Mr. Goggles didn't help with my research. I didn't comparison shop because almost everyone in the country rode mopeds or donkeys. It was just dumb luck that I ended up with one of the best starter bikes ever made. And it had pizazz; compared with the hordes of scooters and mules in the city, I rode a large machine that stood out in a crowd. From zero to proud motorcycle owner, just like that. I loved that little yellow bike from the first rev of its engine on day one. Well, maybe from day two because, truth be told, my friend drove it home from the shop while I sat on the back. "Hung on for dear life" might be a better description, second guessing my madness at every intersection. Even then I was thinking, in a roundabout way, everyone wants to kill us.

Suzuki TS-125, My First Motorcycle

In short, my TS-125 was a peace-loving, happy,

well-adjusted machine. I guess it was a genetic muta-
tion, being a direct descendent of the first dirt bike.
TS-125 would be personable in any environment. I assumed all bikes were like that, well-adjusted, happy
campers.

I would learn the hard way that not all bikes
want to be your friend. Poor selection, or neglect,
will wake an inanimate machine and turn it against
you.

Rule #4: Your Motorcycle May Be Trying to Kill You.

I bought a Honda CR500cc two stroke, single
cylinder, dual purpose bike after necessity forced me
to leave the desert and abandon my dirt bike. I still
think about TS-125. Thumper and I never bonded.

I used simple math to pick out Thumper: with
an engine four times larger, naturally it would be four
hundred percent better. Wrong! Too much Left-brain
thinking, not enough Right. Try four hundred percent
worse! It had a hair trigger and low-end torque com-
parable to a North Korean missile.

Like a slingshot with a hair trigger, Thumper
attempted to rocket me to death on several occa-
sions. No longer riding in a wide-open desert, there
were cliffs, trees, boulders and other natural death
traps everywhere. Unintended acceleration produced tank slap that threatened to fire me, like a
cannon, to my drooling days. Had Thumper been my

first bike, it may well have succeeded in its murderous attempts. Thankfully, TS-125 had imparted just enough throttle control and other physics smarts to save my bacon.

My Second Bike, Honda 500

TS-125's lessons, though, failed to protect me from another murderous motorcycle, Movie Bike, a sassy BMW1200C cruiser built for James Bond's use in the movie, Tomorrow Never Dies. I'm not guilty of *Motorcycle Neglect*; like Thumper, Movie Bike was a *Selection Error*. Looking back, it was an obvious, ill-considered, impulsive choice. I was infatuated by appearance. Physics completely ignored. Too much Right, not enough Left brain. I hadn't been cast in a movie. "Did you think you were Pierce Bronson," Marta asked? I was touring with packs of bikes engineered for covering ground, not posing on movie sets.

My wiser friends rode big road-hugging adventure bikes and other serious machines that glue themselves to surfaces, ready to go anywhere and tackle anything. They built my bike to look good. It whined all the time. "Please, can we stop now? I need to stop. Look: people! Park me, park me! I'm a preening movie star: don't I look good? I was in a movie once!" It liked to get its own way, do its own thing. A rider, admiring Movie Bike, told me, "It's like a beautiful woman. Great to look at, but not very practical." Here's a popular expression you should apply when selecting your motorcycle (or trout fishing rod):

Beauty is more than skin deep. Ask yourself, how is this bike's (rod's) physics?

BMW 1200C Montauk, aka Movie Bike

I gathered with a band of six friends one weekend to head for central Oregon. They, with their tough bikes in a muscled platoon; me driving the equivalent of a lightly armored vehicle made to stay out of the action, toting toilet paper and gun lube for the warriors up front. Stay behind us where it's safe! Despite my riding choice, I tried to go where the pack went. Did what the pack did. It embarrassed me to admit I'd selected a machine incapable of keeping up. "I'll see you there in a few days. Movie Bike has a make-up call and autograph scheduling conflict."

Off the Washington State Ferry in Anacortes we rode, geared up for rain. The sky obliged our preparations and just down the road in Burlington, opened up in a torrential downpour, unusual even for the wet drizzly Pacific Northwest. Determined to traverse the mountain pass to reach our motel for the night in the dry interior, the group pressed on.

In terrible visibility, we entered a roundabout. That's when the mishap occurred. I was distracted (yes, that's a rule for later) by the rain, the traffic, the visibility. Movie Bike, ever the self-deterministic type, clearly wanted to pull over, probably to cower under a tree in self-pity, or snap a pic for Instagram. My mates' bikes easily changed lanes to head for the exit. Their bikes didn't want to kill them; not so true of old Movie Bike.

As it changed lanes, it tripped over its own tires, catching the slippery white dividing line and slipping out from under me in a shower of spray and sparks. It fundamentally misunderstood that this wasn't a time to be scraping pegs. Even the slide it tried to do elegantly, aware of the ever-present mobile phone with instantaneous upload to Facebook or Instagram. Now I'm lying spread-eagled in the middle of the roundabout, stunned and winded and waiting for the afternoon traffic to crush me. But Movie Bike didn't care. Passing motorists gawked from their windows at the celebrity bike made famous by me, ("Bond's the name, James Bond") and pointed at the world's greatest spy sprawled in the middle of a roundabout in Burlington, Washington. "Shouldn't he be in London meeting with MI5? Saving the world from evil overlords?"

Luckily, they didn't run me over. "007 dead!" would have screamed the global headlines. We saved the Queen's tears that day.

I should have been overjoyed, lying uninjured in the rain in the roundabout, but I was rattled and pissed off! "Stupid Movie Bike," I told the guys on their powerful machines, making the obvious point that the fall had nothing to do with my riding skills. I kicked the stricken bike to emphasize the point. Didn't hurt because I had my Lunar Rover Moonboots on. On a GS, I too would have been fine. My friends rallied around–there are many good things about riding in a pack–like them giving the fallen BMW the evil eye, "I told him you were a silly bike. You Harley wannabe!"

The rain eased. We completed some MacGyvering. You know, MacGyver—the guy from the TV series who could fix a broken vehicle with some duct tape and a paper clip? Scratch that... He'd *build* a vehicle with some duct tape and a paper clip. When the bike was fixed, I let myself be persuaded by my packmates not to turn back. Though bruised and recovering from embarrassment, Movie Bike and I travelled south east with the herd, sandwiched between a GS front and rear guard for protection.

I sold Movie Bike just as soon as we returned home. It never completed its deadly mission, but wounded my motorcycle pride.

The point is that motorcycles come in many flavours. Not all are going to be a match, like TS-125. I'm not James Bond; Movie Bike and I were not a suitable pair. Asking a Movie Bike to run with adventure bikes will turn it into Killer Bike. Thumper was too big and way too torquey for the riding I was doing. I had made Selection Errors, and that resulted in bikes with murderous intentions.

In my defence, no one explained that I should be on the outlook for Doctor Doom hitching a ride. I thought all bikes were cheerful, sweet and well adjusted, perhaps with Buddha riding along.

Do your homework. Buy a bike that is appropriate for your skill, size and strength. A motorcycle that is too big and heavy, requiring more pressure to make the bike bend into its initial lean, may kill you. Too powerful for your skill level and the bike will be in control, not you. Royal Enfield, Harley Davidson, Kawasaki, Triumph, KTM, Pliaggio and more—lots of well-engineered choices to make your selection from. Keep your machine in good working order and it will remain faithful. A good-natured dog in the wrong hands will turn into a killer—NOT the canine's fault! Be aware, it's the same with motorcycles. Neglect your bike and it will go from puppy dog to monster, from well-behaved to mauling its owner. Bald tires and dodgy brakes are just waiting for Rule #4 and Doctor Doom to kick your ass.

Dumping your Killer Bike need not be an ethical dilemma. No need to fret about being scolded on Judgement Day if you are a responsible seller. "You're the one who sold a Killer Bike to Mary McGregor, huh? Couldn't you, at least, have thrown in your old, dirty, spare helmet, to protect her bare pretty head? And have forced Martha to put it on before she wheelied out of your driveway?" Be accountable.

The right buyer will tame your bike; cause it to lose its murderous inclinations. Give Doctor Doom the heave-ho. Even make it cheerful. For instance, Movie Bike would be perfect for local TV weather personality, Eddie Edwards. Eddie likes to pose and cruise slowly where he can be seen. Stop and take selfies with fans. Just don't ask, "Any better weather headed our way Eddie?" He hates that. It could cause him to do something STUPID.

Brussels sprouts, for everyone but a few Flemish outliers, are the equivalent of eating stinky, raw, slimy slugs, except they taste worse (Marta warned Tony, she would take MRR's battered pickle order else where, if his deli served a single Brussels sprout). A Flemish connoisseur can take you off the hook. You must find Killer's soul mate. The equivalent of Mr. De Smet, Brussels sprout enthusiast. "Enjoying your raw slugs, Mr. De Smet?" Just like there are sprout lovers, someone is a match for your Selection Error. On Judgement Day, God will congratulate you. "Good job sorting out that Killer Bike situation, Roy. Were you aware the Devil was trying to weasel into its circuitry? Gave up when you sold it to Mr. De Smet. It was exactly what he needed."

The best practice tip below is a tough one. Humans hate to admit mistakes.

Don't nurse a cantankerous bike. Dump it before it kills you.

TS-125 was as far removed from being a killer as it's possible to get. I wonder what became of my capable friend? Hope she didn't have to lug shackled lambs to their death.

I'm wandering, losing my train of thought in a warren of side streets. Time to slap myself and focus. Are you ready for another rule?

RULE #5,
COMPLACENT

I struggled with Motorcycle Riding Rule #5. It's hard to be constantly on the lookout when nothing happens. It's like working as a sentry during peacetime or as a security guard at a Brussels sprout factory. What's the point? What am I looking out for? Who gives a shit? A tree could do my job. Think I'll play on my phone rather than scan for nonexistent threats. One day Radical Dick sneaks up, crawling on his belly in the dirt, rifle strapped to his back, hunting knife between his teeth. He sights the sentry in and squeezes the trigger. Wounds him with his third bullet (Radical never won marksmanship ribbons like his little brother but is a better orator) and then slits his throat. Hello, Flemish-Luxembourger-Prussian Major Conflict! You Never Can Tell when Brussels sprouts will push decent diners over the edge, a starving gypsy will become violently delusional, a North Korean test missile will go off course, or a motorcyclist will slip into Blobland, crash and die.

Rule #5: Complacency Can Kill You!

A truth about motorcycles is: it has its moments of JOY, but they come at the cost of merciless monotony and drudgery. As Marta says: "Sometimes it sucks, and sometimes it doesn't." It's not a surprise. Eating, sex, watching sports or soap operas; overdo anything or make it too bland and humans get bored. Spice it up a little by wearing a tutu while having sex or playing Russian Roulette while watching sports. Boredom produces complacency. Complacency on a bike can kill you (as will, which Russian Roulette falls under Rule #2, Stupid You.) You can learn technique at Parking Lot Cone School but developing a Motorcycle State of Mind, requires THINKING.

#5 wasn't an issue driving TS-125 around Middle Eastern City. Noise, chaos, animal slaughter and human misery kept me constantly alert. No hidden snipers. The odd hidden snake. Killers drove out in the open. Murder by vehicle was a misdemeanor. At times vehicles scared the kebabs out of me. Rule #5 likes that. It keeps you on your toes. It loathes boredom, constantly signalling, "Mr. Dick, over there. Sitting duck in a massive complacency fog! Easy shot! Even Radical could nail this duck."

Prairie grasslands are beautiful but have highways with never-ending straight stretches of motorcycle nothingness, no blaring horns, or dead animals; not even a child ready to dart out from behind one of those trees planted as feeble protection against the wind. Boring. With a capital B. Even Rule #5 falls asleep here. Motorcycles like to go around corners. They deplore straight. You do too. It causes you to switch cruise control on or flip down your throttle lock. Fire up your playlist. Fiddle with the Bluetooth controls on your helmet. Two hours of nothingness since you left the Nothingness Coffee Shop and Truck Stop. *Wasn't this supposed to be outlaw exciting?* You're stuck driving through Complacency Wheatland. A little worried about bored cops, but where would they hide? Suddenly your bike dives into a huge pothole. Or was it a black hole? You were playing with the controls on your GPS when you should have been scanning the highway. Watching for Mr. Dick. You're flung over the bars, like sweet Mary McGregor. Neck snaps. Luckily for you, just paralyzed from the neck down, not brain dead. Thanks to your AstroNut helmet. *Rule #5! Rule #5! Rule #5!* Repeat as often as necessary. It can save your life. It's not a complicated rule. Always, always, BE AWARE. Guard against complacency.

Remaining constantly on your toes isn't easy. Humans are inclined to shrug and give up. I attempted to learn the local language in Middle Eastern city, but my brain isn't a language sponge. In fact, Marta says, "It's more like a bag of wet cement." But it got essential phrases down, added in a bit of sign language, and made do. I spoke at a sub two-year-old level because my brain said, *Fuck this! Good enough. TS-125 doesn't speak the language, so why should I have to?*

My learning came in dribs and drabs. Educating yourself is often like that. Your brain reaches the good-enough stage and coasts. *Fuck this, it's good enough,* it signals! If you're riding or wrenching and hear that phrase, look out. Deadeye listens for those exact magical words.

Yes, you can be motorcycle complacent when you're not on your bike. Maintenance slips. The tires that should be replaced aren't. *Fuck this, they're good enough.* "I'll get to it next year," you tell yourself about the repair job you've ignored. You fail to check your bike before climbing on. What about this bike, Dr. Doom? Seems like you'd be welcome. Step right up and slide into the thingamabob. Conceal yourself behind the whomajigger. Don't forget to wave to Dicky.

The boring fix is throttle up. Pump adrenaline through veins and into the brain. It drives complacency away. Also puts you in danger of violating Rule #2, doing something stupid. See how the Motorcycle Riding Rules interconnect? Marta's working on a flowchart to illustrate the interaction. Big job. Hope she doesn't say, "Fuck it! It's good enough," before she's finished. I'd like to hang her chart on the garage wall, as well as include it in *More Scraping Pegs.*

Also, I mustn't become complacent and forget about answering that other daunting question. What happened to Bob? "Bunny, want to jump up? On my

lap. Any new Bob theories?   Let's do some thinking,
shall we? Or maybe have a nap."

RULE #6, CHOICES

My cat, Bunny, likes his quality time. He's called Bunny because he killed the next-door neighbor's rabbit. Actually, he didn't, I'm kidding—he just likes to sleep in the rabbit hutch with Hammy, a real rabbit who thinks he's a pig. Bunny greets me when he hears the sound of my motorcycle. We sit together in the lab-garage awhile. Bunny sticks his claws in my pant leg and pulls himself up to relax on my lap. Sometimes his claws dig into my skin and I set Pearl, my dog on him. Don't worry. Pearl's a licker.

Bunny's some kind of exotic Siamese, I was told. I don't know. He was "looking for a good home," when I picked him up for free. I was "looking for a good cat" to replace our dead one, Squirrely. I paid more attention to the "free" part than the "exotic" part.

I run theories about what happened to Bob by Bunny. He's very receptive and respectful, unlike my wife who shoots me her, *shut the F up about Bob*, glare. Bunny purrs and massages until he eventually falls asleep. Do cats really sleep? Bunny appears to nod off, but I suspect some part of his brain is constantly on guard. Probably for Pearl, who sulks whenever Bunny and I enjoy quality time. Hammy couldn't care less—rabbits just like to eat and make baby rabbits. They're not good contemplators like Bunny. Especially ones that think they're pigs.

Bunny is what neurologists call a "memory trigger" and I have what doctors call, "a brain that needs triggering." I made a few triggers up to placate my doc. It's one of the "memory exercises" I'm supposed to do but don't. Here's how I explained my Bunny trigger to Dr. Li (to prove I'm seriously exercising):

1. I see Bunny;
2. The phrase, *"There is more than one way to skin a cat,"* pops into my frontal lobe;
3. Sometimes accompanied by horrific images of bunnies being skinned alive;
4. My brain interprets the saying as, there are multiple ways to achieve a goal;
5. And remembers, Rule #6! Rule #6! It's all about making smart choices!
6. Thanks, Bunny!

If your brain is a sieve like mine, consider developing a few Motorcycle Riding Rule memory triggers to exercise your noggin. If you make a game out of it, it won't seem so silly. After all:

Rule #6: Your Noggin Can Save You.

This rule is the flip side of Rule #2 where Stupid You was trying to kill you. Here Clever You is trying to save you. Rather more preferable, right? When your riding buddy goes on a rip in terrible conditions and you're not at your best, use your noggin. Don't chase.

Don't follow that bike weaving dangerously through traffic. Weaving is always dangerous, use your noggin and choose a safer option like knitting (careful of the long needles). Lane splitting where there's no margin–could marginally split you instead. Your buddy nails a tough jump and eggs you to do it too–well, eggs splatter, so make a smart choice; pressured to buy a motorcycle beyond your skill level, but just like your buddies–ask your buddies if they'd like the pressure of that motorcycle lying on top of them in a ditch. Thought not.

Part of using Rule #6 is not allowing others to put you in a position where you may be killed. Reject dangerous peer pressure and showmanship. You're no army recruit following Loo-ten-ant Foolish Dan on a suicide mission. On this occasion, what your mother told you was right: "Just because Amber drives her bike like an out-of-control meth freak, doesn't mean you have to! If she rode her bike off a cliff, would you follow?" Maybe back in the day. But now you don't use meth, you use your noggin!

Rule #1 embed the fact that you're in a war and everyone is trying to kill you. Think of #6, your noggin, as the commander of your *Zone of Awareness*. Looks like DD is behind the wheel of that black pickup truck (#1). Better watch the front wheels (#6).

You can see how #6 has a ton of applications in your *off-motorcycle* life. "Or," Smart Alec Marta likes to ask, "Maybe you're perfect? Like Gandhi or Trumpie and don't need to be reminded to use your noggin?" She's being facetious, of course. We discussed how Gandhi choose to always walk, rather than ride a motorcycle; absolutely not a smart choice.

Marta calls #6, "The No-brainer Rule," because, "It's so obvious." But it's not that simple. Think of it this way: did you ace the big calculus exam back in junior high? Unless your name is Sir Isaac Newton, probably not. Every question on that exam had a factual answer. Answers within the grasp of most human brains. If you had used your noggin effectively, you wouldn't have flunked. Today you'd be an astrophysicist instead of battering pickles for Tony at his deli. Noggins require discipline. Many don't like to do calculus. *On-motorcycle,* you must always do the math. Keep your coconut dialed-in. Maybe a coconut would be a good memory trigger for Rule #6?

"#6 reminds me of Movie Bike," Marta stated bluntly, before biting a battered pickle. "You were guilty of not using your noggin and doing something stupid. I hope you don't do that in the lab. Maybe it wasn't a Killer Bike after all?"

Thanks for pointing that out, Marta. Yes, I followed, failed to act, even though I knew it was unsafe. The rules interacted and Movie Bike tried to kill me. Should I blame myself for not Using My Noggin? Or for being Stupid? Here's an important tip, especially if you're a deeply sensitive cat and dog owner like me, dealing with tough questions from the Marta's of the world:

> *If you're involved in a preventable and embarrassing situation, like I was with Movie Bike, where the incident can be traced to multiple root causes, ALWAYS pin the blame on the Rule that doesn't make you look like a complete jackass. That's using your noggin!*

"Definitely a Killer Bike, Marta. There's more evidence than just the roundabout story." Did she buy it? No, but Marta understands how sensitive I am and has learned to respect my feelings. Mostly, she's concerned about a snack budget cut if she goes too far.

Bunny understands. I insisted Marta include my cat and dog in the snack order. She agreed with this condition: dependent on Tony lowering the Lab price of battered pickles. She wants a free pickle for every six purchased. Seems fair. Tony countered by offering to double the loan period for *A Brief History of Time* (but the Lab would still have to purchase the Cosmic Special to qualify for the book loan). "It's a bit of a pickle," Marta said in her update. I suspect they'll reach agreement after a motorcycle ride.

Motorcyclists are a diverse bunch. Cruisers,

sports bikes, scooters, trial bikes, adventure bikes, sidecars, touring bikes. There is more than one way to skin a cat, remember? Take Classic Bikers (CBers). They keep the past alive, nursing their aging iron horses with noggins that use old school thinking. Bikes that others look upon as scrap metal, CBer brains somehow turn into show pieces. Tradition is important to this respected group of two-wheel historians. Masters of machine tools. Possessors of sage-like secrets and coconuts exploding with knowledge. Their bikes must be rewired, or the carburetor cleaned, during each group ride, but they use their noggins and get it done. They're off Deadeye's radar much of the time because they're busy cleaning up oil leaks or machining valve seats. They all have a copy of *Zen and the Art of Motorcycle Maintenance*, but not one has managed to get past page nine.

Classic Bikers and Zero SR or S1000RR riders sit at opposite ends of the motorcycle spectrum. Today's machines are filled with wizardry. No pulling over, unwrapping the small tool kit that waits under the seat, and using your noggin to overhaul the engine. No foil across contacts or cranking that oversized adjustment screw to be on your way. Today's machines can't be fixed without a software patch and the secret tools Service keeps locked away. No wonder classic and modern bike owners come up with different answers to the same question: how to stay alive on a motorcycle. Both climb on alone. In the saddle, they THINK, but their well-balanced brains produce dissimilar instructions, conditioned by history and technology. One swerves right, the other may brake. One is not right, the other wrong. On a motorcycle, *there is more than one way, and plenty of wrong ways, to skin a cat.* Your noggin must produce its own split-second decision. Motorcycling isn't like that junior high calculus test. There is more than one way...

Don't want to use your noggin? There's a three-wheeler for you. How about a self-balancing two-wheeler? Just kidding! Of course, you must use your noggin on a Can-Am Spyder and God help you if you have a sidecar. "If you want a noggin test," Marta suggests, "Jump on an old Guzzi or an BSA Rocket 3."

She's right. Motorcycles have become more complex, but easier to ride. Technology's progress has reduced brain load. There's trickery in modern machines. It's an unintended consequence of engineering excellence. Old BSA Rocket 3s came with built-in reminders to keep you alert, your ass pounding, your fingers numb, and your noggin yelling, "Enough! Pull this stupid contraption over. Please, let's tinker with the carburetor for a while. Get me off this damn bucket of bolts! It's given me a BSA of a head ache!"

Let's be very clear, I'm not blaming engineers for making modern bikes riskier, but easier to enjoy, thereby tricking riders into believing their bike will do much of the thinking for them. No! Rule #6! Rule #6! Use Your Noggin. Listen up:

Don't blindly rely on your motorcycle's capabilities, make use of the computer in your head! Rule #6! Rule #6! Your smart bike can't always save you!

Are modern bikes too clever? No! Riders must absorb Rule #6 and stay in the game. Motorcycle engineers know how to get to solutions. If there was a, Using Your Noggin Ceremony, our engineers would be on the gold medal podium.

Most riders know this. They step off their bikes and unavoidably fall into the world of political theatre—from near perfection to perpetual looming disaster. "Shouldn't we be using our balanced brains to run the World," Marta asked? "Who decided letting screwballs run amuck is the right way to run a planet?"

"Us," Tony answered. "Voters."

"But," I pointed out at the deli (I'd come to support Marta's battered pickle campaign), "Politics... political science, is a closed loop. Do you suppose Sir Isaac could win a nomination race today? Not a hope in hell. Zero Newtonians at political nomination meetings. A few balanced brains may ride to the hall, but most will bail long before the vote. There is not a Party of Pragmatic Thinkers because balanced brains have all figured out that politics is a pragmatic wasteland." *Pie-in-the-Sky? Oh, you want one of the Pixie Dust parties. Just down the hall, one on the left. The other on the right.* I don't point this out to mock or denigrate my PolSci friends. It's no secret their discipline struggles with common sense. "Right Brain Syndrome, I'm afraid, Marta. Nice folk and terrific talkers, but don't expect many well engineered solutions. Not their forfeit."

Marta's kicked off a project to develop a political science, balanced brain, solution. It involves box eels and a trip to Bali. Tony's deli supplied free battered pickles at the inaugural meeting, "Because it's a worthy cause and it was just Marta and me."

There is a simpler solution. Ask motorcycle engineers for help! Quit arguing about the seating plan for the *Political Science Summit* in Bali and seek assistance! If political scientists outsourced their responsibilities to motorcycle engineers, the engineers would perfect the base platforms from which societies flourish, in no time. From stable bikes to stable societies, both with auto-correction features for Blockhead operators. It's an obvious solution, but if your unbalanced brain gets tripped up over seating arrangements, like they say, "You can't see the wheel for the spokes." Apologies to the few balanced brains who successfully slipped into the political arena. Can't imagine how frustrated you must be.

Because motorcycles are considered toys to our overseers, cycle engineers fly under the radar. An outsourcing contract wouldn't raise an eyebrow or be treated as serious news on our networks, unless it's discovered that one of the engineers knows a racist, anti-Semite, misogynist, xenophobe.

This Save The World scenario came to me while I was riding in Tennessee and thinking about Marta's box eel solution. As I've said, motorcycles are terrific Thinking Machines. They fire up both sides of your brain. Produce moments of Absolute Clarity like replacing political scientists with motorcycle engineers. And risk mitigation lawyers with political scientists (why not throw them a bone)? I'm not vindictive.

Marta came up with the box eel idea while riding her Guzzi. She'd like to trial it on a city council early next year. Any volunteers?

If you happen to be in Tennessee, switch MRR to High, and ride the Tail of the Dragon—enjoy 318 glorious curves in 11 miles. Don't think about saving the world. Just ride. Isn't that what motorcycles are for? Escaping reality? "If reality is political theater, is reality really reality," Tony wanted to know?

I shrugged and said, "Use your noggin, Tony." Marta wants me to play hardball until there is movement on the battered pickle front.

If you're contemplating buying a motorcycle for the first time, think: Noggin! Ask yourself, do my left and right brains get along? Does my coconut become perplexed when this question is raised—where should people sit? Am I way more political scientist than motorcycle engineer? Does my brain perform mostly single-sided operations, which, on a motorcycle, is deadly? Look at the mess political science has made of the world and transpose that to driving a motorcycle. Not a pretty thought.

As part of her project work, Marta looked up the on-line definition of "political science." We had a good laugh. "Political Science is thus an organized body of knowledge the facts of which have been scientifically and systematically observed collected and classified and from these facts are formulated and proved a series of propositions or principles which form the basis of the science."

"You'd think, with a job description like that," Marta said, "They'd be able to organize getting a few bums in chairs." The scary thing is, some political types ride motorcycles. "Which is worse," Marta asked? "A Blockhead, SQUID, or politician on a bike?" The Lab will look into the question as well as this one: will a political career eventually erode a balanced brain to the point of making motorcycle riding unadvisable?

We've gone around the mulberry bush a few times, contemplating Rule #6. There's a touch of political science in us all, we shouldn't be too smug or self righteous. The essence of Rule #6 is simple: use your brain to make smart choices (you see how politicians are ruled out?). Defining how "smart choices" are arrived at, in a split second, on a motorcycle is complex. If you're still baffled, here's a suggestion: find a Classic Biker and talk it through. Offer to polish their forks while your brain gets polished.

Broaden your perspective. Your noggin will be better equipped to save you when it must make a life and death decision in half a second.

The cat's back. "Find anything tasty in the yard, Bunny? No? Well, let's get you some food then." Oh-my. My memory trigger has been, well… triggered. Sometimes the mechanism works too well. I can see bunnies being skinned alive. *There is more than one way to skin a cat…*

My Cat and colleague, Bunny

TAILOR THE RULES

"**A**BS for the mind," Marta calls the Rules. Once absorbed, Awareness and Ability are always on the job, never interfering with JOY. You may have to give yourself a metaphorical slap in the face occasionally to ensure your brain is on the job, but that's it: you can twist the throttle, ponder, and do all the things you love to do on your bike. Be an outlaw. Pull off the road and have sex, but not with a goat (more about sex and goats coming up). Scrape your pegs. Feel the rhythm of the road. Drop easily into one bend, accelerate out, and set up for another. You'll be tempted to quit your job and keep riding. What's over the next hill, I wonder? Let's find out.

Deserts have rolling hills with uneven surfaces instead of a confined amount of smooth blacktop like a parking lot school. There are no cones to avoid and no need to wear a high-visibility vest. No instructors standing around with clipboards making judgment calls. There are natural berms to jump, hills to climb, and learning opportunities to explore in every direction. Deadeye has nowhere to hide. The riding surface is forgiving if you go down. No gear pressure; blue jeans, a long sleeve shirt, sneakers and an open face helmet with a sunshade will do. A way to carry water is all the luggage required. When I was comfortable flying fearlessly, at full throttle toward a berm to achieve maximum air, I graduated.

Learning to Ride

In Middle Eastern City there's an unwritten law —the police throw the book at expats regardless of fault. Foreigners in vehicles are always in season. It's part of the pact you agree to in exchange for living abroad. Here Rule #3 has a subclause: *You're always at fault, you foreign imperialist pig-dog. Pay up! Or else!* Generally, it's unwise to choose, or else. But if you're on a large 125cc, highly maneuverable bike, possess desert riding skills, and don't comprehend what's going on, do you ride like there's no tomorrow? Past the musallah where the adhān bellows from a speaker on the minaret of a mosque. You've watched the movie, The Great Escape?

Is it a wonder I eventually took to Curmudgeonly Jackass-ism? My parents tried to do the right thing, attach me to a religion. I wasn't keen on spending Sunday mornings dressing up, listening to hymn music, or kneeling, while struggling to survive. Even as a boy, Motorcycle Church would have been a far better option for me. Ride a minibike. Perhaps with Buddha? In the fresh air. Christ, You're very welcome to tag along. But no kneeling or preoccupation with sins and damnation. Let's do Sunday School my way.

Church works for many people, and that's a blessing. Curmudgeonly Jackass-ism works for me: no services, collection boxes, crusades, jihads, bad music, and no rules about not using technology, like motorcycles. Bob and I used to joke about this being one of our teachings; "The Truth is out there." We stole it from the X Files.

When I told Marta, she said, "Yeah, but you jackasses won't find it." The rest of the teaching goes, "Buried under a rock." It's kinda like *Buddha lives in the circuitry of your bike*, except with a rock. Deep, right? We laugh when we say it, which isn't often because we don't hold services. It's an Absurdism. Most religions take theirs very seriously. I've never clued Marta in about the rock part. She thinks we don't have a clue where the Truth is.

Remember my idea about motorcycles being mandatory for world leaders? Let's extend it to include religious leaders. Talk about getting closer to God; jump on a Husqvarna, Kawasaki, Vespa, or your favourite bike. Peace on Earth through motorcyc-ling! God be with you and with your motorcycle. Exodus 19:1-25. God called Moses up Mount Sinai and gave him the Ten Commandments *after he parked his dirt bike.* Stop looking for the ark. Use a metal de-tector and find the divine dirt bike. God only pro-vided half a tank of gas. Moses couldn't have gone far.

No need to include Curmudgeonly Jackass-ism in the religion decree. We're not a religion. Most of us ride and are busy looking for Truth under a rock.

Religion is a big deal in Middle Eastern City. So is traffic, slaughtering lambs on side streets, and swindling naïve travellers. Car drivers deal with the congestion by flashing their headlights and honk-ing their horns incessantly. Lambs don't comprehend that we intend to turn them into kebobs, and tune out the craziness.

Fathers often carry their wife, kids, and four or five chickens or a goat on their moped. The physics of moped loading. I never understood how they man-aged, but it was clear the family had a lot to lose. For them, Rule #1 is: *Everyone is out to kill me, my family, and my next meal.* Inshallah, God willing, it won't hap-pen.

It's OK to tailor the rules to suit specific cir-cumstances, like being a moped dad. They're univer-sal, but most people will have an oddity or two to deal with–go ahead and incorporate them. Don't be blindsided because you didn't apply the rules to your situation. For example, you could expand #2 to remind yourself of a particular vulnerability: Don't Kill Yourself by Doing Something Stupid *like riding home from the bar, you drunken, pathetic fool!*

Tailoring isn't a rule, but permission to adapt. After I explained my Tailoring Memory Trigger, Dr. Li said, "It's nice that bikers have taken an affirming perspective." I was happy she liked it and I wasn't coming across as a complete Neanderthal. Here's how this one works:

1. Turn on a TV news channel;
2. Wait no more than four minutes;
3. A sexual rights story will air;
4. When it does, the name Taylor Templeton pops into my frontal lobe;
5. Sometimes an image of Taylor getting pounded also appears (both scenarios);
6. My brain makes the connection, it's okay to Tailor the Motorcycle Riding Rules.

Back in the day, before it became trendy and fashionable, *out of the blue*, Taylor Templeton came *out of the closet*. That's why my brain automatically links the sexual rights revolution to Taylor and then to Tailoring. "You see how you can put an old, ingrained injustice to good use, Dr. Li?" I'm pretty sure Dr. Li would say I've taken memory trigger therapy to a whole new level.

SEX AND MOTORCYCLES

Motorcycle mommas, rampant outlaw rape, and pillaging parties are relics of a bygone era. Some would say, "Too bad," but the fact is, motorcyclists are not misogynists, masochism, rapists, sadism, anti-liberation Neanderthals. We suffer from the same set of lust afflictions as the clergy, Congress, parliamentarians, steelworkers, kindergarten teachers, and all humankind, except Whirling Dervish Dancers. Marta agrees with my position on motorcycles and sex, but warns, I may be influenced by, "Repressed Mary McGregor fantasy baggage."

Personally, I don't give a rat's ass if people are nonbinary, leaning toward pansexual, a good old-fashion homosexual like Taylor Templeton, or uncertain and experimenting. Just stop waving those holier-than-thou rainbow flags and droning on and on about it, please. Look at us, we're special and misunderstood! No, you're not! That ship has sailed. Nobody cares, so shut the fuck up! A custom chopper is special. You're not! We're busy trying to find the truth about motorcycles. You don't hear us droning on and on about it and getting endless media coverage.

If you're older and have scars, like Taylor, you're likely on drugs and sobbing in a corner, but if not, and you want to let loose, okay. Try to be brief and to-the-point. Also, buy a motorcycle and go for a long ride. It's the best possible therapy. Study the Rules first.

Are you opposed to same sex shenanigans and anything goes attitudes because of a deeply held religious belief? Fine by me. That's your prerogative. But keep a lid on it. Please! God will hear you out when it's your turn. Be patient. You'll be on deck right after followers of Curmudgeonly Jackass-ism, carrying the Truth they found under a rock.

Yes, the truth is out there, motorcycling is LGBTQ compliant. We have all your major persuasions covered. Dykes on Bikes, to name one well-known early adopter. Sure, we have sexual nay-sayers and our quota of deviants and predators, we're a diverse bunch. Everyone in the LGBTQ community is a saint, right?

Sexually frustrated? Buy a bike and go for a ride.

Buy into the hunks-on-bikes folk lore? Talk to Marta.

Had it pertained more directly to riding; this would have been a rule:

Motorcycles don't care what adult sexual flavours you experiment with, out-of-the-saddle. When you're riding, there are more important things to get your feathers ruffled about, like staying alive.

◆ ◆ ◆

Before I went globe trotting, I secured an international driver's license. I thought it might impress the ladies. Just kidding. I knew I'd need a snazzy motorcycle to do that.

Off I went, into the congested playground of Blockhead drivers, camels, donkeys, goats, and the odd snake, calling back over my shoulder to foreign spectators, "I'm not nuts! I'm a motorcyclist!" Could have added, "I'm a member of an increasingly LGBTQ compliant group, by the way." Young Middle Eastern City heterosexuals couldn't hold hands in public, let alone explore diversity. Want to lose your head over sex? Sometimes it's best to keep your mouth shut, your ethical positions in your back pocket, and your motor running.

GOODBYE TS-125

I hauled shopping bags of groceries, one dangling from each handlebar to equalize balance, in accordance with the laws of physics, home to my apartment in Middle East City (I had yet to learn Rule #2, Don't Kill Yourself by Doing Something Stupid). I toured, got out of the chaos for solo overnighters. No cell phone, tire repair kit, tools, GPS, luggage other than a backpack, or biker attire. Despite the lack of those, and my minimal local language skills, I had cheerful TS-125, Mr. Dependable, who never let me down. Thank God! It didn't dawn on me then that motorcycles have problems that leave riders parked in Dire Straits. I was lucky to have an unbreakable, faithful companion. Otherwise, I'd have been deep in motorcycle doggy do-do.

My circumstantial development went well. Learning to ride, owning a bike that didn't want to kill me, Rule #1 locked in, and good luck brought me home intact. My rookie riding experiences were smooth as silk, with just enough frayed edges to teach me I had more to learn. Without knowing it, I had been living the riding dream the industry and popular culture promote. Life really is marvellous on two wheels! I fell in by complete accident and everything slid into place. Not the bike though; that stayed upright, no sliding there—mostly. Despite my naivety, the motorcycle gods took care of me. I returned home whole, ready to nod knowingly when I read *Zen and the Art of Motorcycle Maintenance* for the first time. Is this fact or fiction?

Many North American riding years were banked before, out of the blue, Deadeye locked me his sights and squeezed the trigger.

The Truth About Motorcycles is:

No one, including YOU, is immune to the rules that govern motorcycles!

PART 2 - HOME AGAIN

RULE #7, BE STUBBORN

My riding euphoria came to an abrupt halt. I suffered motorcycle-less shock. Sun and endless desert exchanged for west coast rain forest coupled with other riding deterrents, like family and mortgage. I dreamt of TS-125, but that page was turned. The Thumper replacement was attempted, but that Killer left me mourning my past riding life even more.

Here I was, listening to local biker chatter, trying to figure out why reasonable people, living in a miserable riding environment, rode. Even stranger, why are they fanatical about it? *Don't they know any better? Riding in shitty weather, on roads, is not the way it's meant to be. Am I missing something?* We swapped stories, enjoyed biker conversations. I offered a few TS-125 tidbits. The bikers were polite but quietly dismissed my cheerful little bike as a toy. "Oh, you've never ridden a real bike," they asked? "Real," meant at least 500 pounds. Even Thumper wasn't a real bike. They owned big bikes. Proper road machines. Unlike riding in the desert, size matters on the street.

Mostly they told riders getting themselves out of trouble stories. Laughing off shitty weather tales. The bull moose on the highway. The cop that nailed them, "But not at the speed I was doing a few minutes earlier!" I wanted to share my, *soldiers in the shoot-to-kill pose followed by a die-you-foreign-pig-dog interrogation story,* but it seemed unrelatable in the rain forest. They talked of running out of gas and almost running out of gas. The semi that turned into their lane. Wind blasts on the plateau.   The mattress on the road before the turnoff. Most of all, they looked forward to their next trip. I didn't know it then, but these veterans had developed a thick skin that easily allowed them to apply Rule #7:

Rule #7: Be Stubborn in A Good Way.

Don't whine. Deal with consequences. Be Accountable. If a life action happens, *on-bike,* like rain, be a soldier. Not even foul weather, that keeps sane people indoors, stopped my new friends from riding. To my amazement, they spent fortunes on wet weather gear and heated grips. They ventured out in less-than-ideal conditions and found JOY. I thought, it's not right; I hadn't yet absorbed Rule #7.

In the desert, #7 wasn't a big deal. The climate and terrain obliged motorcycles. Even the traffic was a predictably unpredictable and a free form dirt-bike riding adventure. I was young; there was no toughing it out. Never had to dig down to make the next stop.

Listening to experienced western riders, I learned about new challenges, like miles of monotony, rainstorms, speed traps, bad gas, flat tires, gravel, traffic jams you cannot ride around, and tight corners. How rational perseverance is your friend. Don't go off half-cocked with steam coming out of your head. That's Rule #2, Stupid. Avoid #2 by being stubborn in a good way. Maintaining balance on two wheels is essential.

The word, "stubborn," sometimes makes me wonder if Bob flew into the Thompson River just to prove he could. Was he that bullheaded? *Bet I could fly half way across. Kick off my Lunar Rover Moonboots and swim out. Collect insurance, including the boots.* Bob would say something like that, but never do it. *Good plan, Bob. When you gonna do it?* Now I'm not so sure. Maybe he would do it?

Home with my pretty useless Desert & Chaos Motorcycle School Vaporware certificate, I read *Zen and the Art of Motorcycle Maintenance* for the first time, as well as *Jupiter's Travels.* Watched *The Long Way Down* and the *World's Fastest Indian.* I dumped Thumper, just as Dicky loaded the Killer Bike rule into his sniper magazine. Now I opted for a string of low budget, progressively larger street bikes. I was moving on with my motorcycle education, but still had a thing or two to learn. Three, to be exact, if you're using the ten Motorcycle Riding Rules to count. I absorbed #7, and it kept me on the Road to Joy.

RODE TO JOY

J OY keeps riders climbing on. Maybe a Zen master can define it, but I can't. For me, it's too nebulous and rider dependent. The JOY that Extreme Ape Hanger Guy experiences is certainly not the same JOY Rosie discovered on Pink Lady. It can be the serene peace of a comfortable steady ride on a long, picturesque and winding road; warm sun and cool breeze and a cold beer at the end of the day. Or scrambling up a hill smoothly. Riding toward decaying ruins in the desert or sighting a camel formation, like a caravan of old. Leaning into a curve, scraping cruiser pegs or accelerating out on a sports bike. Perhaps one day I'll be able to define motorcycle JOY. For now, please use your own definition.

The clock ticks on. At this time in the narrative, I'm no longer alone–now I'm sharing life with my two kids, a cat, as well as my wife, Dori. The sprawling desert of exploration and rider training has gone; so, has the perfect cheerful bike. I've dumped Thumper. Now all I have is yet another in a string of mediocre bikes. It'll-Do-Bike, better than no bike at all, but it would never be the gorgeous red Ducati in the poster stapled to the garage wall behind it. I wonder if It'll-Do-Bike was embarrassed? Thoughts of revenge, *I'll become a Killer Bike!* What if I'd stapled a Mercedes coupe poster behind the shitty, dented family sedan?

It'll-Do-Bike never tried to kill me, but neither did it teach or inspire me. In short, I became a Part-Timer; the sad decline of a once former glory.

These are the things that turn motorcyclists into part-timers: familial responsibilities; the steady march of time that makes hours on the bike a bit uncomfortable; work, life speeding up, leaving less time for JOY; the bike you get on OK with. Oddly, wild lunch-hour discussions about the cross-continent motorcycle odyssey we dreamed of doing one of these years, also had the opposite effect–instead of riding more, we rode less, as if banking time for the big trip; just heading out for a Saturday afternoon jaunt felt somewhat pathetic by comparison. Why bother? May as well wait for the epic ride. The more chatting we did about our version of The Long Way Down, the more we stayed put at home. When you're young, all-or-nothing attitudes persist. They gradually wear down to, just a bit will do.

"We" were a makeshift group. Five work mates loosely bonded by motorcycles and a corporate culture. Riding was a luxury; we should all have been working, mowing lawns, getting in shape, taking the kids to soccer, changing the oil in the van, fixing that loose tile in the bathroom, returning borrowed tools, repaying Aunt Edna that overdue loan, taking a course, or bonding with our partners. We didn't get out often. We were trapped by life, not in charge of our time. But life still painted pictures of freedom and escape on two wheels.

For most of the year, our low-budget, ok-but-not-great machines waited, lonely and ignored, left undercover or in the garage to collect dust. They waited like statues, reminders of a past glory. "Why don't you sell that thing? Trade it in on a carpet cleaner." Once a year, for three glorious days of summer, we'd attempt an escape. Sometimes successfully. Often compromised.

We'd loosen the bonds, throw off the shackles of responsibility and take off on a brief but monumental ride. An abridged odyssey. Eagerly anticipating the short parole, we'd cash in our Get Out of Dodge cards (the riding would be good, but the escape would be awesome) and plan our adventure. Brush up on the Motorcycle Riding Rules, at least the ones we were familiar with. Up would roll the garage doors with the sunlight spilling in to show just how much grime the garage and our bikes had collected. As I sat wiping the dust off my bike, my thoughts drifted to Peter Fonda and Dennis Hopper in the 1969 movie, Easy Rider–like them, I was heading off across America. Just without the drugs. Or the proceeds from cocaine sales. Technically, we were in British Columbia, not America and only going part way across one province. So, not really like them at all. Motorcycles are great for that. They transport you from one reality to another, like boarding a jet and stepping off on the other side of the world.

Our escapist, eclectic group of riders assembled. We wrapped our legs around steel like TV cowboys. Our two-wheelers polished and snug between our thighs. *Nicer than your average It'll-Do-Bike*, we fooled ourselves. In our minds we were freedom fighters, but everything about us shouted "Part-timers!" A motley crew of weekend warriors with slapped together, bungy-corded luggage and make-shift riding gear that the Beemer Bunch with their superior machines and perfectly accessorized gear would snub their noses at. Our bikes as makeshift as our gear: an older Harley, a variety of Japanese brands and styles–nothing matched. Obviously not credible enthusiasts, having made minimal investments in second-rate technology.

Except for Ninja Guy. No braces for his kids, because he has no kids. No alimony either–you guessed it: because he never married. With money to spend, he'd done his research and splashed the cash on a formidable machine that wouldn't hold back. Looked like he'd stepped off a motorcycle billboard. He was a threat to be taken seriously. A student of Physics Rule #3, regularly attending track days, camouflaged within a pack of part-timers, Ninja Guy would do our talking. "Look at him go! No one takes Ninja Guy. He's with us," we'd shout from our It'll-Do-Bikes. Truthfully, though, the rest of us didn't care: part-timers out for an escape, not for a race; oblivious to motorcycle envy and neurosis. You tell yourself that because you know It'll-Do-Bike doesn't like to race, you could do something stupid, or find yourself on a Killer Bike.

Just wait till I get the red Ducati in the poster on my garage wall!

We rode east day one, away from the ocean and over mountains that fell to rolling grasslands and ended as desert in the interior. Not the arid, barren desert I had trained in, with its endless pathways of sand, but one covered with sparse, low-growing shrubs and divided by barbed wire fencing. Barely enough sand to remind me of past days. Now I rode on a ribbon of asphalt.

Perfect weather: sunny and comfortably hot. Three o'clock put us an hour from our planned overnight stop. There would be beer, a meal, some exploring, and many tall tales. We rode through orchard country, past fruit stands, gradually descending into the valley and roads that run beside long deep warm water lakes. Apples, peaches, apricots, and cherries. We looked forward to climbing off and resting our bodies. Snacking on fresh cherries. Drinking beer. Reliving the day's ride. Joking about the discomfort of cherry diarrhea. Talking about how Ninja Guy smoked the poser on the white and black bike.

We travelled under a blue sky but, in the dis-

tance, a rebellious storm waited. An ominous darkness threatened to engulf us. It became a race. Would
we make our motel before the menace in the sky
caught us and let loose on our shitty make-do, probably not water resistant, work wear Dennis Hopper
outfits? We sped up. It was the best strategy we could
come up with.

The storm appeared lost. Out of place. Not in
our plan, meticulously scheduled to coincide with
good weather, but here was a small renegade, a developing weather system, surrounded by bright blue
summer skies. We were ill-prepared for the unpre-
dicted looming confrontation.

The dark sky faded on each side, from black and
threatening to light and inviting. What was behind
it, we couldn't tell, but we rode on a collision course
with what was visible.

It began with thunder. Thunder that shook
the ground beneath us and radiated up through the
frames. Our thighs and legs pressed against steel, taking on its strength. We leaned forward, closer to the
engine, and felt its power. High energy bolts of lightning followed. We moved in awe toward this spec-
tacle of nature, not twenty miles west of its grandeur.
Thunder shook us as the sky exploded; it was otherworldly and indescribable. The motorcycles made
us vulnerable participants. We rode toward nature's
power in front row seats, marvelling and fearing its
consequences. There was no alternative but to con-

tinue, fully exposed but drawn toward wonder.

We rode for twenty minutes, feeling the anger, strength, and glory, watching the orphaned storm's holy splendor, knowing God must have a hand in it. There could be no other explanation. Perhaps there is more to life than Curmudgeonly Jackass-ism?

Then the rain began. Light warning drops at first, quickly turning into a downpour. Stubbornly, we persisted. Ready to tough it out, hoping we could be stubborn enough. Just after the rain began, a fruit stand, with a covered seating area, appeared like an oasis in the desert. The store was decades old, waiting by the road in exactly the same spot, year after year. It was as it should be, but to us, it was a mystical apparition.

We climbed off, shaken. Moved by our shared experience, bombarded by, and in awe, of nature. No hugs. We didn't break into a chorus of Kumbaya, or swear in an excited, exaggerated way about what we'd experienced. It wasn't necessary. "It is what it is and it ain't what it ain't."

We waited in silence, strong men. Bikers. Not outlaws, but tough. In the hands of God. Our It'll-Do-Bikes and make-do luggage tested by His storm or whatever you ascribe the realization that, *there-must be-something-more*, to. **The Truth About Motorcycles is: they can reveal a Glimpse of God**.

After ten minutes, kickstands up; we rode to

our motel under clearing skies, giddy men, a band of brothers unified by an extraordinary phenomenon, one we'd never be able to share with others in a way that would do our hour of JOY justice. The encounter renewed my affection for motorcycling. It didn't matter that our bikes were shitty, or that we were part-timers. Our motorcycles made the experience possible, and we thanked them for it. It wasn't about skill, technical capability, or money, it was about being in the right place, at the right time, exposed. It was one of those rare events impossible to describe. "You had to be there," one of us would say. The others would nod, yup, you had to be there.

And there's the rub of it: you really had to be there. Sometimes you go for a ride and JOY finds you; once in a while a trip leaves a memory that refuses to fade, and these offset the drudgery that motorcycling can be. It's why we ride. It's a truth about motorcycles. "Sometimes it sucks and sometimes it doesn't." To get there, often you have to be stubborn in a good way. That stubbornness means living with the reality waiting for you as you step off your bike, because all motorcycle trips inevitably end and life naturally picks up where you left off. There is joy in the daily living as well—I love my family. But now and then I sneak down to where the garaged It'll-Do-Bike rests and stare adulterously at the red Ducati poster. Have a beer and dream about owning the road with Ninja Guy. Kitty always sneaks in just before I close the garage door.

I look at It'll-Do-Bike and smile. *You were there. You know, right?*

Every road can be an adventure. I understand why people love to ride in their environment, whatever it may be, even on an It'll-Do-Bike, like the ones I've owned.

I have never owned the red Ducati in the poster, but I have had more extraordinary moments, sandwiched between hours of, well motorcycle dullness. **The truth about motorcycles is: there is both JOY and Tedium. Sometimes there is Misery and a Glimpse of God.**

DOLDRUMS

The Oil Years followed, the It'll Do Bike Years. Oil is part of biker vocabulary, like, "How you likin' this weather? How about that sports team?" When you run out of subjects, the question is; "How you likin that new oil?" Or, "You think'in of going full synthetic?" These are the conversations of the Oil Years. Nothing much happens. "How you likin' this weather? Which oil filter you use 'in? Wax or sealer? Mid grade or high octane?" The doldrums.

When my kids were approaching adulthood, I bought a used BMW R 1100RS. I figured it was time for something more than, It'll Do. That's how I met Bob. "Top speed, 140mph," were the first words he said to me. His ride was a V-Strom 650, newer than my bike. He was thinking of trading it in. "Maybe on a RS." He liked the idea of the oil head boxer engine.

We became motorcycle friends only because I owned the bike Bob had his eye on. Had I been riding something other than an RS at the time; we wouldn't have hooked up. Bob wasn't gregarious and I'm socially lazy. We didn't have kids who played on the same sports team, similar occupations, nor did we live in the same neighbourhood. We clicked, even the part about curmudgeon killjoys not having a sense of humor, but mostly we talked motorcycles. Even oil at times, though we were not passionate. Had it not been for my RS, we would never have hooked up.

I think of my teal R 1100 and Bob as a pair. Introduced to both at the same time, they helped me emerge from my motorcycle doldrums.

Like TS-125, special bikes come along from time to time that fit perfectly into your life at that moment in time. Teal RS was one of them. It was a coming out bike. Out of stagnation. Fortunately, I'd brushed up on Rule #3 (physics) because RS liked to race. Looking back, I was lucky Deadeye didn't nail me, leaning and twisting the throttle on my 1100.

I continued to ride happily until the crash, several bikes after R 1100RS.

PART 3 - THE LOTTERIES

RULE #8, YOUR NUMBER

I often see lottery winners on TV holding up over-sized cheques: perplexity, confusion and elation written large across their faces in equal measure. "I'm going to give up my shitty job and travel!" they shout at the interviewer.

I yell back, "And buy a bike, you idiot. Even better, buy me one and I'll come with you."

Winning big lotto money is always unexpected. That ticket, bought along with a small bag of peanut M&Ms, and a tank of gas, just like the hundred times before. Except on this day, despite enormous odds, the numbers came up. It was "out of the blue!" winners loudly remind the interviewer on the obligatory TV spot.

Would you please stop shouting! The interviewer puts on an, *I'm so happy for you,* professional smile. *Tickled pink.* The question that perplexes the interviewer is: Why do assholes always win? *Trying to make me feel bad, are you? Always the interviewer. Never the winner*. Well, Mr. Interviewer, the saints are busy saving the world. They don't have time, or money, to squander buying lottery tickets. Winnings should go to the gamblers. To buy a motorcycle and fund their habit. Is Gandhi going to buy a motorcycle? No!

Dumb question, Mr. Interviewer: "Were you surprised?" Of course, they were–the odds are astronomical, and it's not like they did anything to help themselves. The winners would have been overjoyed to win a free bag of M&Ms. I know I would; beats the cheap Chester's Locks promo key chain I won ten years ago.

Sometimes I hear, "I so love my job and my colleagues and my little desk and the potted plants by the toilets, so I'm gonna keep working. What would I do if I didn't work?" WTF? Why did you buy a lotto ticket if you don't want change? You really are a jackass! Tandem brain's first thought ALWAYS is, MOTORCYCLE. Buy one to go with your peanut M&Ms. Even better, buy me one. Have I said that before? I can show you the way, if you're able to keep up.

As a famous actor once said: "Life is like a box of chocolates: you can always purchase a motorcycle and a copy of *Scraping Pegs* and head off on an epic adventure." Yes, he really said that. Or was it Marta at the lab? I remember Steven Wright, the comedian, once made this observation, "When everything is coming your way, you're in the wrong lane." He virtually quoted Rule #8.

Rule #8: Your Number May Come Up

Having the greatest day ever? Doesn't matter. With Rule #8, when they reach for your number, there's duck all you can do about it. No time to duck. It's motorcycle's Dirty Little Secret.

DIRTY LITTLE SECRET

The Motorcycle Lottery is not organized like the club door prize draw where they make a big production out of gathering everyone together, at a specific time, to give away swag. 7:30PM - you're staring at the number on your red ticket, hoping to win the coveted key chain from Chester's Locks. "Everyone, check the number on your red ticket. Only the red ticket. Who's going to be our lucky winner tonight? Let's give Chester, from Chester's Locks, a big hand for his generous donation."

If the Motorcycle Lottery was like the club door prize draw, you'd hear, "Okay riders, get on your bikes and go. Dicky will do the honours and pick one of you bastards off. Who will our unlucky rider be today?" Here are the facts:

The Motorcycle Draw is always Under the Table and Out of the Blue.

That's the deal with Dirty Little Secrets: people are aware they exist, but they're vague. Kept on the down low and the hush hush, like Nazi extermination camps and the Brussels sprout special at Agnes's Flemish Bistro.

Usually there are bits of the other rules mixed in with Rule #8, like Rule #1 (Everyone is Trying to Kill You)—lady runs a red light, blows a tire, and crosses the center line to hit you head on. Sometimes it's out of a horror movie—those unsecured metal pipes falling from the plumbing truck in front of you, the open utility hole cover, or getting caught in the cross-fire of road rage. The key differentiator is speed, Rule #8 happens so fast, you're unable to take effective evasive action. Deadeye's shot is a certainty. It's this simple: to climb on a motorcycle is to enter the draw. The ticket's free and no-one is excused. Not even Mr. or Ms. Really Expert Rider, who believe they're exempt. Timing is a mystery. Calamity is never expected.

When you pick up your bike at the dealership, the salesperson doesn't say, "And here's your free lottery ticket. Hope you don't win!" Nope, it's all about wind against your new helmet and the JOY that awaits down the road. Marketing types constantly work to suppress the existence of Rule #8, but you know it's there. Don't you? Maybe around the next bend or right in front of Chester's Locks?

SQUABBLE

Thanks to Marta, there was dissension about #8's validity. "How can an event which a rider has no control over, be a rule? A tire flies off a Mach truck. Nails a bike like a torpedo. That's a rule? C'mon! It's out of the blue and there's bugger all to be done about it," Marta argues. "Can't be a rule. It will undermine MRR's integrity." I understand her skepticism.

What is a rule anyway? A rule is an instruction you follow—it guides your behaviour. I can hear you thinking, indeed if you weren't thinking it, you should have been: I've struggled with this question myself. As Marta stated, "#8 is fate, not a rule." Let's address this seed of doubt.

The answer came to me in Wyoming, as I rolled toward Salt Lake City. Long motorcycle rides are perfect for resolving perplexing questions. There were many matters to be considered besides the integrity of #8. I put Marta's challenge aside to wonder, will I find Aprilia's and Harleys parked at the Tabernacle and witness Mormons on bikes? If so, Joseph Smith and the Church of The Latter-Day Saints might be onto something. Does the Book of Mormon contain answers not revealed in the *Zen* book?

Ok, truth time–I wasn't really committed to investigating the Mormon–cycle proposition, but I pondered the possibility on my long ride. Eventually I decided, fuck it! Good enough just to see the Tabernacle. No need to explore faith's connection to inanimate objects. I'm no Robert M. Pirsig. I was leading you down a dusty detour there.

Alright, alright, full honesty: I wasn't travelling all that way to see the Tabernacle either. I was actually going to the 2017 MOA BMW rally, not on a mission to investigate the symbiotic interaction of man, God, and motorcycles. Just going to take part in a two-wheel cultural-commercial exposition. Like Sturgis cut with water, starch and German Königsberger Klopse. Now that is the God's honest truth. I figured; I'm in SLC, may as well take in the big church, as one does.

That's all there was to it; I really was travelling across the grasslands when I alternately contemplated #8's validity and do Mormons ride? Now that I recall the trip, I was also dreaming about the great cowboy breakfast in the town of Rock Springs. Drop by if you're in the area, you know where to go now. I did, and what a brilliant decision!

That's really all there was to it. In a nutshell, I was riding toward Utah in order to reach SLC and attend the MOA rally. Full confession, the rally was merely an excuse to hit the road. I barely "attended." Basically, I needed a break from Marta's constant badgering about #8. She can be so tenacious. And that's why I had plenty of time to think.

I really did deliberate, alternating between #8's validity as a rule and do Mormons ride? Over a thousand miles in the saddle, you know what it's like. The great morning meal in the town of Rock Springs also replayed in my mind. I was getting #8 straight in my coconut, taking my time, enjoying the coffee, then a second cup. When I considered a third cup, it hit me–I was stalling. Not that I was afraid–heck, no, I love biking; I love it so much I'm writing a damn nonfiction book about it instead of the one Marketing wanted, filled with outlaws, whores, and motorcycle chases. No, what I mean is that the prehistoric medulla-hypo-meta-whatever in my brain was unconsciously realizing that when I left the café, and got on the bike, I would be back in the Motorcycle Lottery. My number may come up. Since the cafe was cozy, the breakfast tasty and the coffee strong and sweet, my primeval brain was urging me to keep my ass safe and secure in the chair. That's the thing about dirty little secrets. Every so often they like to poke up and remind you, you can't hide under the covers forever.

Eventually I climbed on and rode off. The medulla-hypo-meta-whatever in my brain settled down. I enjoyed a moment of Absolute Clarity.

Since my stalling was a behaviour, therefore, from our earlier definition that rules guide behaviour, #8 must be a rule! Hallelujah! No wonder the folks at MRR Labs eventually listen when I speak. It's not just because I control Marta's snack budget.

I was so excited; I almost wheeled around and pointed my bike back to Rock Springs for a second celebratory Cowboy Breakfast, but the travel allocation (from Larry's donation) was running low, so I didn't. "Capital preservation," the financial folks call it.

I can hear philosophy graduates applauding my logic; the motorcycle engineers vociferously disagreeing while insisting Rule #8 is pure random chance and demeans the value of the actual rules. "Why don't you just attach a roulette wheel to your rule book?" I respect their point of view, sort of, and agree to disagree. For a second opinion, I asked the PolSci crew working at the fast-food place. Last we spoke, #8 had triggered a heated exchange on the potential discriminatory effect of rules in a pluralist society. Whatever that means? Hello, right brain to planet Earth. But they were able to serve a barely edible chicken sandwich.

My defence of #8 continues: not only is behavior affected before the rule comes into effect, but also afterwards. You're riding along, thinking, the world is my oyster, and it happens, out of the blue. Whamo! Your number comes up. If you're dead, which is twenty-six times more likely in a motorcycle accident than a car accident, end of story. If you're not dead, there are the years of painful physical rehab, counselling for panic attacks, feeding your free PTSD service dog, and the loss of friends as you retreat to your bedroom and discover the local dealer delivers. Sure, that's worst case, but either way, #8 affected your behaviour. Rules influence behaviour, remember the definition?

You may agree with the motorcycle engineers and label it, "pixie dust and fuddle-duddle," but my Wyoming decision stands: Your Number May Come Up remains a rule, cemented in the eighth position. And scrub those suggestive, *where I can shove #8*, scribbles off the MRR Labs unisex garage washroom wall! Charge the cleaning supplies to the Snack and Washroom Maintenance Budget. Don't touch my travel allocation, Marta!

MORE DISCORD

Marta is a very smart cookie, but sometimes...

With reluctance, Marta eventually conceded that, Your Number May Come Up, can be a rule, albeit somewhat of a lame rule. But, like Lenny, she doesn't know the meaning of, silence is golden. *For the love of God, Marta. Enough already!* "What's that?"

"You heard me. Why's it at Number Eight and not Number Ten? Out of respect for common sense and order, it must be the last rule due to its finality! Your number comes up — Finito! No need for more rules! Your goose is cooked. Full stop. Did you throw a dart at a board to arrive at #8's position? Talk it over with a bovine in Montana?"

"Glad you asked, Marta."

Actually, I wasn't at all pleased. Smart people can be such a pain. Robert M. Pirsig never would have finished his maintenance book had Marta been around to badger him. Ditto for Professor Hawking. "You really expect me to believe that black holes just popped up, out of the blue?"

The position answer is simple, Marta: #8 provides hope of continuing on to #9 and #10. The two remaining rules wait like lighthouse beacons, spreading symbolic rays of optimism. To modify a well-known greener grass idiom: "the road is always curvier further on." There is evidence of survival beyond the blast site—former riders, living their decrepit lives, some with free service dogs. "Hope is so very important, Marta. That's why *Your Number May Come Up* is staying put where it is. In a word, HOPE."

"Battered pickle?" So, like Marta to change the subject, rather than to say, yes. Makes sense.

DIE TRYIN'

When I won my Chester's Locks key chain, it occurred to me, maybe that's my number drawn and done with. I won a cheap promotional key chain instead of a transformation, but at least the odds of my number resurfacing are minuscule. Thank you, Chester! It proved not to be the case but,

Hope Springs, Eternal.

Not that I know where Eternal is and aren't springs for damping? Or is the morning meal in Hope Springs better than that of Rock Springs?

HOPE is that nebulous visor flicked down when riding to give everything a rosy-tinted glow. It says all will be well, regardless. Motorcyclists will not be browbeaten by Risk Management Guy or intimidated by the odds of going down. Even when Rule #8 fires from Deadeye's rifle, there is HOPE.

My cousin Len is a Motorcycle Lottery poster boy. A survivor. Although it's good Len's still around, one-legged but more than capable, the downside is, he continually yammers on and on about his stub to anyone who'll listen and boy, does Stumpy like to talk about how my fat auntie nailed his Yamaha.

Just like some folks can't stop talking about war. By the way, it's nice that the Japanese and the Germans both did a 180 after WWII: their countries now make excellent motorcycles which spread JOY around the world. "Don't forget the Italians," Marta adds.

I wonder if any motorcycles survived Hiroshima? If they did, were they safe to ride?

People say this about me; "You're about as empathetic as a lab rat. For a shoulder to cry on, I'm going down the hall to Marketing where the caring folks hang out. You have no sympathy for one legged cripples or Hiroshima victims." Wrong! Just because my sleeve says, *cry me a river asshole* rather than *compassionate warmth found here*, doesn't mean I'm cold-hearted. Ever hear of strong, silent, semi-Newtonian types? Remember, I own a cat? Bunny, and before that Squirrely. And a dog? Pearl, and before her, Opal. I'm an Honorary Copley Park Dog Mom, for Christ's sake. Plus, I brought Len a potted plant when he was in the hospital. My sister Barb advised me, "I'm sure Lenny will appreciate a nice plant." He didn't. Didn't even ask what it was. I was prepared; "Spider Plant." Guess he's not a deeply sensitive nature and animal lover like me. Plus, I'm against war and dropping bombs out of the sky unless absolutely necessary—they may land on motorcycles. Besides, there has to be a better way for a country to develop motorcycle design and manufacturing expertise.

I must ask my cousin; did you ride long enough

to feel JOY? The few moments of elation that keep you climbing on? The vibrancy of the extraordinary mechanical beast beneath, twitchy and responsive; its proud parent-like engineers watching from the banked corner you've just nailed, saying, "We've done our jobs well." Or ambling along a serene country road. Maybe dodging a traffic jam feeling like a million bucks? JOY can happen anytime, anywhere. It's a product of uncaged wheels. Here's the thing:

Motorcycle JOY is what they call "nebulous." MRR Labs has been unable to pin it down, although we suspect it has to do with weather, the absence of car doors, twisty roads, no cops, little traffic, and great engineering.

Lenny was a bit of a Blockhead. Doubt he made it beyond noisy pipes and *Born to Be Wild* blaring from shitty speakers. Too bad.

My friend Larry's death was definitely joyless because he's one of those who went through life *without motorcycle*. He wasn't even doing anything stupid the day he died. His sickly, depressed, fatso colleague stuffed down an entire box of Larry's crackers without a problem. He was so absorbed with his cracker binge; he didn't notice his business partner choking to death on a single cracker. When asked how it happened, fatso shrugged and said it was, "Out of the blue." I could never convince Larry to give motorcycling a try because, "I don't want to die." But he did. Crackering. Nevertheless:

Don't encourage friends to take up motorcycling.

*They may win the Motorcycle Lottery. Then family mem-
bers will torment you. Uncle Wacko may attempt to run
you off the road.*

Guy Clark has a song called Die Tryin'. I like
to think it's about Motorcycle Riding Rule #8. If a
motorcycle takes you out, at least you died tryin'. If a
cracker takes you out, well...

The flowchart Marta's working on diagrams
lottery relationships. If you're alive, you're in the
Death Lottery and like Larry, your number may come
up served on a cracker. Works the same way as the
Motorcycle Lottery, but it's not a dirty little secret.
We expect to die. Nevertheless, like the people of
Hiroshima, it can come as a surprise. Animals are
blessedly off the hook. Otherwise, life, for many of
them, would be a giant holocaust. Instead, they ride
the slaughter truck to the abattoir without a care in
the world.

You can't withdraw from the Death Lottery,
but the Motorcycle Lottery? Dump your bike, buy a
tank. Or stay in bed. But remember, shit happens in
tanks, beds, and Hiroshima too. Drop by the garage;
I'll walk you through the flowchart. It does a nice job
illustrating how everything ends in Death, but not all
Life Paths create JOY.

It's a safe bet that the same outfit operates both
the Motorcycle and Death Lotteries. The draws often
work sequentially. Number comes up in the Motorcycle Lottery, there's a good chance you'll kick the

bucket at the same time. Another mystery in need of resolution, WHO runs these lotteries? Start your search at the tabernacle in Salt Lake City. Or at the Vatican. Mecca? Or Lotto Central. Rock Springs? Doesn't matter, but please get on it. When I looked, I didn't find any Illuminati, just a bike shop selling those LED driving lights that are way too bright. Actually, I wasn't looking—just another lame excuse to go for a ride on the Lab expense account. The travel form Marta created requires, "Purpose of Trip" be filled in.

Lottery timing is an enigma, although if you're ninety-six, had a heart attack, have no health insurance, and were wheeled into the boiler room next to the morgue, it's a safe bet, your number is coming up. Same thing: if you're cranked up on Bennies, don't have MRR, and decide to see if your friend's Panigale will really do 130 mph / 210 km per hr.

Let's wrap this up. We've beaten #8 to death with a stick. Rule #8 is valid because:

Behaviour. I've laid out how #8 can modify behaviour. Yes, it's a metaphysical argument and motorcycle engineers aren't on side, but too damn bad. Political scientists may weigh in one day and validate my position.

HOPE. There is a reasonable chance you'll come out of the Motorcycle Lottery draw battered but alive and perhaps get a free service dog. Without HOPE, why bother learning the other nine rules? #9 and #10 provide anticipation of more to come.

Preparation. Housekeeping is important. Use #8 as a reminder to ensure your insurance policy is paid up, your underwear is laundered before travelling, your will is up to date, and generally to do those things referred to as, polishing your grave stone.

JOY. Taking care of business, thanks to Rule #8, will allow you to ride easy, knowing you've done everything that can be done. "It's in God's hand." Nothing more to do except cruise over to Rock Springs to enjoy the Cowboy Breakfast.

PART 4 – HEADING OUT

RULE #9 & 10, GOATS

I left home, Victoria, British Columbia on August 16, 2019 with my riding buddy, Conrad. Both of us on BMW F800 GTs, mid-sized touring machines. Mine, white with a small custom teal accent; Conrad's, dark graphite. We were experienced riders; older, not stronger, skilled but trying not to be complacent, a bit slower to react but not as impatient. To compensate for the slippery slope of age, we had both moved to smaller bikes. The F800s are forgiving; they have the knowledge of generations engineered into them. They know a thing or two about what to do and what not to do. Put a competent, experienced rider on a capable bike and you'd think the odds of their number coming up would be minuscule. Especially ones who have MRR in their back pockets. But like they say, you only need one entry to win.

On I climbed and into the draw I went.

My GT

Between us we had over fifty years of injury free riding. A couple of bumps and scrapes, but nothing too dramatic. Conrad's most recent incident occurred on the American plains a year earlier. A wild turkey damaged his bike. Insurance took care of it. A duct tape and tie wrap repair job got him home. His number came up, but thankfully, it was the equivalent of winning a shitty door prize. No big deal. The unfortunate thing is, Rule #8 doesn't go on hiatus because you walked away with a minor prize. Nope: fire up the engine and your ticket goes right back in the draw.

My previous mishap took place on a roundabout north of Seattle, Washington on Movie Bike, remember? Movie Bike was a Killer. We discussed how whining, or weather, or any irritant can get under your skin. If your MRR isn't strong, you can lose control and a bad bike becomes a killer. A single irritant can lead to death. Like hot, stifling weather, or a large buzzing thing caught in your helmet—for a second or two, it drives you mad. In your madness, you make stupid happen. You get the idea, so here's Rule #9:

Rule #9: An Irritant May Get Your Goat

Rule #9 has implications beyond the obvious meaning that "to get your goat," is "to drive you mad or cause you to flip out." The hidden, the silent, sardonic part is.... *And the Goat Will Kill You!*

Rule #9 is important to guard against. A chunk of kryptonite and suddenly, there's hell to pay. An Irritant May Get Your Goat triggers another rule, then it's goodbye yellow brick road. Repercussions. Rules interact. One thing leads to another. Radical Dick taps his brother on the shoulder, "I've had it with this duck. He's getting my goat. You're a better shot, Dead-eye." Dicky raises his sniper rifle and fires. Thanks to Radical, another duck down.

Marta illustrates all this in her flowchart. For those of us who learn best with visual aids, the diagram is a blessing. It's almost finished. A donation to the Lab's battered pickle fund, would put it to bed.

Being asked to donate can be irritating. Don't allow something that aggravates you to fester and grow. When you're visiting the in-laws, or attending that event you didn't want to attend, it can be next to impossible not to let a bug crawl under your skin. But in these situations, you make use of a coping mechanism such as heavy drinking, tapping, or whirling Dervish dance. On a motorcycle, it's just you and your noggin. You must develop a Motorcycle State of Mind to clear your mind. Don't climb on and go to war bent out of shape over a bad relationship, who ate the last battered pickle, or whose turn it is to change Bunny's litter box. Anger will cloud your judgement and get your goat.

One irritant may not get your goat, but two? You bite your tongue while chewing gum, which hurts like hell, right after having the Cowgirl Breakfast you got talked into when you really wanted the Cowboy Breakfast. That breakfast sits niggling in your stomach as you crawl behind the annual RV parade, right at the best section of the highway. Damn breakfast choice! Horrid gum! Bastard RVs! All the while watching the low tire pressure indicator and wondering if the next part of your day has you stranded with a flat. Finally, cracking through your disgust, you spot an opening and roar past the parade. And smack into the side of the first RV that's turning left out of the parade line and into the well-signed Rendezvous in the Forest site. The gum caused you to bite your tongue, irritating the hell out of you. You did something stupid and Rule #2 leapt up and bit you. Yes, there was a goat involved, but it's complicated.

RV turning out? Well, it... turns out... that a goat blurred your vision, and you missed all the banners. Turns out that disgust started with a bitten tongue. Turns out, you shoulda let it go and got over it earlier. Turns out, that one irritant got you good. If only you'd spit the gum out. The stupidity of biting yourself.

Let's clear the decks of goats before carrying on. There's only one rule left and we've touched on it already. We'll put them all on the table as Conrad and I hit the road and get to the good part of the book, the crash. Here it is, the end of the list, for now.

Rule #10: The Multiplier Effect is Also Trying to Kill You

An irritant, (we all have an Achilles' heel), can pick a rider off. Often these mistakes or distractions are not huge deals in and of themselves, but they escalate, one on top of another. Frustration levels rise and accidents happen. Don't tell Marta, but I really added #10 to address her nitpicking accusations. She likes to go on about how all the rules work together and I shouldn't single one out. "I believe you're taking about the Multiplier Effect Marta. Rule #10."

One time, I forgot to put my magnetic tank bag on properly after gassing up my Concours. I was thinking about what an asshole my boss at the time, was. The bag came flying off and landed on the street when I pulled out of the station. A SQUID move, but not a game changer. I put the bike on the stand and went to retrieve it, but tripped as I went. Another jackass move. I went sprawling. If you'd been watching, you might even have called it a decent looking

fall, as I did a tidy barrel roll when I landed, though
I didn't appreciate scratching my helmet. But I rolled
too far... and landed in front of oncoming traffic. It
was moving slowly, thank goodness, but it had rained
and the road was slippery. The nearest car saw me,
slammed on the brakes and skidded in slow motion
towards me. I didn't have time to move and ended up
with my hands on the hood, staring in semi-horror
at the equally terrified driver. One foot more and I'd
have been knocked over. Five miles an hour faster and
the cars behind would have rear-ended him. As it was,
they'd been able to stop in time. The multiplier effect
had kicked in and I was lucky to escape. I glimpsed DD
laughing at me and waggling his finger, saying, "You
can't always be so fortunate, Jackass."

"Just wanted to retrieve my bag, Dick," I explained. "Must you always be so damn trigger
happy?"

"It's what I do. My job. Part of the fabric of life."
Dick can be opportunistic.

Another time, one of my bugaboos happened:
a large, pissed-off, stinging insect became trapped in
my helmet, very much alive. It buzzed like a killer
drone, unable to escape and furious. You would be
too. Flying along, minding your own business, and
suddenly you're sucked inside a stinky hell hole with
no way out. My gloved fingers were essentially useless. Panic levels rose as I waited for the creature to
drill into a fleshy part of my head, perhaps my eye-

ball, blinding me. I was travelling at a good clip with nowhere to pull over. My goat's barely under control. Despite the extreme buzzing, I'm not over the edge into madness. But teetering. Suddenly, there are other tasks to perform besides pest control. Passing. Braking. Signalling. A car over the center line. The multiplier effect was kicking in BIG time.

You should know: I escaped that time as well. The Mexican Killer Bee, which it turned out to be, having eluded the border wall, had safely snared itself in the padding of my helmet. I dodged the straying car, passed the slowing truck, signalled my intention to change course and braked to a halt in a driveway. My heart was pounding faster than a Van Halen song. Slowly, it returned to normal. I took my helmet off and flicked the killer away. Did Dick send it? To do reconnaissance?

That's what it's like with the Multiplier Effect. One problem's manageable, never causes a huge issue; not your kryptonite. Some days, though, they pile up and added together, become too much. Two or three goats can combine to take you off the Road to JOY. You lose the ability to control the situation, giving Deadeye a clear shot. The Multiplier Effect is one sneaky SOB.

Here's a Best Practice Tip to help you cope with one or more goats:

When dealing with goats, do the opposite of your initial reaction; don't twist the throttle and drive like a possessed Blockhead in an ill-advised attempt to outrun them. Instead, release the throttle, pull over, and let the goats wander off.

CONGRATULATIONS!

Hallelujah! Take a bow, dear reader, and soak in the applause. You've completed your indoctrination. Now gas up, get on, ride out and end a day of JOY sitting beside Buddha above a mountain pass, breathing glorious fresh air and thumbing through a copy of this book because repetition is essential.

If you're experienced, perhaps more experienced than me, you may be saying to yourself; I knew this stuff already. *In fact, I know it all, have pretty much done it all, and don't need some jackass telling me how to ride.* If you're a know-it-all, as I can be, that's a natural reaction. It's okay! I'm not offended. I told you at the start, this stuff can't be packaged and sold as a YouTube video magic answer. The Rules remind you to THINK, but it's up to you to develop Awareness and Ability.

Also, there are no MRR certificates, like the ones they award Parking Lot Cone School graduates, although Marta has suggested offering seminars with a diploma. Proceeds going to the Box Eel Solution Development Fund. For an additional charge, take home a copy of the flowchart. Perhaps with a free battered pickle if Marta can work a deal with Tony. I'm hesitant because, if we hand out MRR Certificates, and students fail to develop their Motorcycle State of Mind, and then crash, folks will say, "This certificate is no damn good," instead of, "This rider is a Blockhead."

Learning to ride and staying alive are processes. They're not like brain surgery where you get a degree, a handshake, and you're good to go. "Here's your hammer drill and diamond bit set. Remember, drill into the cerebellum only where you see the red laser dot." Motorcycling isn't brain surgery, it's fluid; there are no red laser dots to guide your way.

The rules we covered so far have been pretty straightforward, right? Except maybe the brief parts about metaphysics, calculating atomic weights, and understanding dramatic license. Professional educators say, "Key concepts are foundational to lifelong learning." Motorcycle engineer trainees must nail Newton's force and energy before applying for professional accreditation. They are encouraged to "cycle through," to test validity as they continue to develop and advance their craft, always falling back on key principles. Political science students must... well... do what that definition Marta read out says. A better example; if you want to do calculus, first nail arithmetic. Maybe not a great present-day example. Was it Bill Gates or Steve Jobs who said, "Fuck doing calculus? Let our computers do the math." But you get the idea?

So, take *Scraping Pegs* out from time to time and review the rules. THINK! Reinforcing learned behaviour is critical. Just for fun, develop some memory triggers like Bunny and Taylor Templeton. Don't let me down now: practice your technical riding skills and be aware.

Want to celebrate completion? Grab a drink. Let loose with Die Try'in or a John Prine song or a Georgian chant.

Don't suppose there's a song in the *Time* book? Let me know because I didn't make it to the end of the professor's "academic book." Mostly because I didn't make it to the beginning either. Tony, at the deli, told me, "There're no motorcycles in it." It's proclaimed to be a profound scholarly yet accessible work. Come on, how can a history of time not include motorcycles? Makes absolutely no sense, right? What about Moses' dirt bike? Without time to sit on a motorcycle, do black holes really matter?

At least Robert has motorcycles in his *Zen* book, even though the part on maintenance is pathetically weak. By the way, I read *Zen and the Art of Motorcycle Maintenance*—also no song. I may add an appendix on valve adjustment for those of you, who like me, purchased Mr. Pirsig's "maintenance book," looking for something a little less intimidating than the engineer's shop service manual, only to find it's Zen Maintenance for Political Scientists. It shouldn't be necessary to point out deficiencies in acclaimed books, but I want you to feel good about the cash you shelled out to purchase *Pegs* over *Time* or *Zen*.   Cash you could have used to buy a nice farkle.

Finished singing? Kickstands down. Relax.

PART 5 – THE CRASH

BORDER CROSSING

Conrad and I had logged thousands of uneventful motorcycle miles. No injuries. No unrideable bikes. Our young and daring days survived and behind us, a mere shadow in the rearview mirror. Now more balanced, we were better equipped to smell the roses and wait for appropriate stretches of road to demonstrate our proficiency and knowledge of motorcycle physics.

Nothing much gets our goats anymore. Call it one of the few advantages of adding days. We weren't SQUID or young desert riders when we left home in August 2019. Old in the sense of been there, done that. Survived. Had to be doing something right. Many more riding years to come.

You're thinking, "nothing much" is secret code for a festering irritant sure to unleash a goat, result in calamity, and punch up a boring story about rules. Is it a hint of a twist?

What is it about an innocent sentence that will immediately have readers suspecting, there's more to this trip story than meets the eye? You're thinking: trouble brewing under the covers? A dirty little non-motorcycle secret? One of the guys has cancer? No. Will the two jackasses end a close friendship in fisticuffs at a truck stop wrestling match? Perhaps he's leaving the spouse... The spouse is leaving him? Money problems? Pet to put down? Kid turned out to be a freak? Conrad secretly enjoys Brussels sprouts? Those annoying squeaky brakes? Who's turn is it to pay for coffee? A difference of opinion over the value of rules in a pluralistic society? Something is afoot. It's sure to get under their helmets and alert Mr. Dick. DD is always on the lookout, but you'd be wrong about the goats.

This is a non-fiction academic book, remember? More like *A Brief History of Time* than an Agatha Christie or John Grisham mystery novel. It's life, based on actual events. Reality with motorcycles and a song, not nebulous black holes and no rules. Down to earth, unlike Steve's *Time* book, which takes place in the cosmos, wherever that is. Motorcycle engineers say Steve's book is more arcane than *Scraping Pegs* (yes, that's a well-deserved compliment). Political Scientist use the word "scholarly" to describe the professor's book and written by a "jackass" to describe *Pegs* (yes, another compliment). Steve was a brilliant thinker. It boggles the mind to contemplate what he may have conjured up had he spent time *on-motorcycle*. Maybe an *In-depth History of Time including Motorcycles?* Let's agree, opinions can differ, but clearly both *Time* and *Pegs* are important "academic" works and Conrad and I were easy going, going easy, nothing getting our goats, no irritants floating by. No mystery novel subplots. Where's Bob? At home. I invited him, but he, "Had a conflict and couldn't make it."

JOY, come on in! Nothing was in our way.

I should warn you, full disclosure: my number was coming up. And the prize would be more consequential than the key chain I won years ago (Marta says it's insulting to win giveaway shwag as a prize which actually made me a loser, not a winner). Obviously, it wasn't "tits up," to use a trashy fiction novel term.   Not all the way to the Final Destination, but certainly resting in the parking lot just outside the entrance to the Valley of Death. If it was Finito! clearly, I wouldn't be wheeling into MRR Labs to check on new rule development or the proposed appendix on valve adjustment. Perhaps I'm more like Stephen was? Confined to a wheelchair but still capable of writing a respected academic book?

It's important to be clear. Before you read about what happened, let me tell you again that absolutely nothing was interfering with the peaceful JOY of this particular ride. It was one of those trips you'd describe as "smooth sailing," or "a walk in the park," or "nothing at all getting your goat." No mitigating circumstances led to my disaster. It was uncomfortably hot for a few hours, but that's nowhere near enough to make me flip out and kill myself. I'm a former heat-of-the-desert rider, remember? Frying eggs on a rock, fifty miles from the nearest palm tree.

The August weather was perfect the day we left. A two-hour ride north, from the southern tip of Vancouver Island, to catch a ferry to the mainland, near Vancouver. We'd ridden the BC-Washington circle route many times. There would be no surprises, nothing we weren't prepared for. Conrad had added wild turkeys to his cautionary watch list, and I'd absorbed knowledge by dumping Movie Bike. This would be a laid-back cruise through spectacular scenery and varied landscapes. A routine getaway, not an odyssey. Neither of us looking to find ourselves, or a lost land in a far-off place, or to morph into weekend outlaws. Just a short, pleasant cruise with possibly a bit of scraping pegs along the way. Nothing extraordinary. Buddha able to relax comfortably in the circuitry of our GTs and partake in our JOY.

With MRR running solidly in the background, we avoid Complacency Swamp and slap our noggins if we think *I'll take a little siesta through this boring stretch.* Like a mobile speed camera enforcement agent, Mr. Dick likes to lurk in the most unexpected of places. We know you're there, squatting beside those other dicks. We're constantly scanning.

We added a few appropriate adjustments to the rules; nothing that would justify a rules committee review, just little extras, like *leave early, stop early,* and *don't eat at joints that serve Brussels sprouts*. Who said you can't have fun? This isn't Medieval Albanian Literature 101 or a Brief History of Time with a complete absence of motorcycles! Yes, an academic book can be fun! It doesn't have to be "the sky is exploding! We're all going to fall down a black hole and implode!"

The ride up the island to catch the ferry is scenic, which compensates for the strangle hold the risk folks have on this section of the Island Highway; it's slow, full of cops and littered with road safety engineering designed to prevent caged Blockheads from being Blockheads and pegs from being scraped. An hour and a half of ocean cruising and we're on the mainland, the Sea to Sky Highway. We rode pass Whistler Resort, host to the 2010 winter Olympic ski events. As I was on a Thinking Machine, of course I had a skiing revelation. A moment of Absolute Clarity. Skiers fly down mountains, uncaged. Ninety miles per hour. Wearing helmets and special gear. Remind you of motorcycling? Exactly!

Like riders, skiers deal with forces constantly trying to kill them. Do they have a book of rules? Definitely. The International Ski Federation Marketing Department capped their rule book at ten and disguised the rest of their rigmarole as "regulations." No skier has been bold enough to step forward and insist on full rule disclosure, unlike MRR Labs, which has Rule #11 in development. Except for minor differences, like noise, athleticism, snow, and boldness, skiing and motorcycling are identical (ski boots are even larger than the clodhoppers motorcyclists like to wear).

What I don't get is, why are these two twin passions, cultural opposites? Buddha hangs out in motorcycle circuitry, but what about ski boots? Where are the skier outlaw gangs and the Hell's Angels Ski Clubhouses filled with drugs and prostitutes? Do skiers not hit the slopes to get over horrific life incidents? Is there a fringe helmetless ski movement? Why is there no après motorcycle tradition with wine and fireplaces? How come the cultural images of bikers does not apply to skiers? Why do nearly identical activities have such different personas?

Skiers will never figure out the answer. Even if they read the *Zen* book, they'll still be scratching their coconuts. Motorcyclists have the immense advantage of jumping on Thinking Machines and riding until they have a moment of Absolute Clarity. Skiers have pieces of carbon fibre epoxy strapped to their feet, gliding on snow which freezes the basal ganglia, preventing meaningful thought. Just before the town of Pemberton, BC, the distinction hit me: *Motorcycle riders are bold free thinkers. More open minded than skiers. Skiers shelter in confined areas, at certain times of the year, unable to move beyond ten rules. They have not evolved to the same degree as motorcyclists. Mr. Pirsig did his research and choose not to write, Zen and the Art of Ski Waxing.*

It was worth passing Whistler to get this gem straight in my noggin, never mind the magnificent scenery and motorcycle JOY. There may have been more cultural perceptions to unpack, but Conrad interrupted my pursuit of logic with an equally insightful comment, "We can stop at the next café for a bite. They don't serve Brussels sprouts."

"Alrighty," I replied through the intercom. Then wondered, do ski helmets have internal comms too?

The GTs wound through the snow-capped mountain valley, bordered by emerald lakes, to the start of a must-ride motorcycle highway. Highway 99, Pemberton to Lillooet, BC, known by locals as the Duffey Lake Road, has magnificent scenery and a two lane, twisting, old fashioned, secondary highway taking riders through low mountains from the coast to the hot dry interior. The perfect start to our four-day jaunt. No need to remind each other, it doesn't get better than this!

There are secret must-ride roads scattered on every corner of the globe, I'm told. They're secret, so I can't be absolutely certain. Despite the secrecy surrounding this stretch of Highway 99, as *Pegs* is a down-to-earth book, I have an obligation to the facts, and am therefore required to state where on August 16, 2019, Conrad and I were scraping pegs. No, we weren't up in the Cosmos, we were on the Duffey Lake secret motorcycle road.

Respect this disclosure, please–we're not fellow magicians revealing the mysteries of each other's illusions. Don't get the locals up in arms! If I'm able to return to the Duffey Lake road one day, I don't want to see a sign that says: "No Jackasses!" because readers took it upon themselves to make a mockery of "secret." I don't want protestors outside my garage carrying this sign: "Thanks for Wrecking our Secret Road, Scraping Peg Assholes!"

Unlike Scotland's Secret Bunker, a widely known decommissioned nuclear command centre turned tourist attraction, now doing a tongue-in-cheek disservice to the word "secret," secret motor-cycle roads are genuinely obscure. You are welcome to go to the Secret Bunker–it's not a secret anymore. The Scots will sell you a Secret Bunker coffee mug and a Secret Bunker tee shirt. Motorcycles welcome! Take a, "I Visited the Secret Bunker" sticker for your Triumph. Warning: now that it's no longer in the nuclear business, you must pay to park. When the Newtonians ran it, the lot wasn't a "revenue generating opportunity" but the Secret Bunker Marketing team changed that.

Scots wear kilts without boxers, drink scotch by the gallon, play a mean bagpipe, eat haggis, and deep-fried Glaswegian Mars Bars (yes, you can buy them at the Secret Bunker). Marta tried one and reported, "They could make a killing selling something edible, like battered pickles." But the Scot's true testament to boldness was operating a nuclear command bunker. It's like waving a flag, "Over here, Mr. Nuclear Annihilation Dick!" Finito! Scotland.

As I was pondering the differences between secret motorcycle roads and secret nuclear facilities, and placing Scottish Boldness ahead of Skier Boldness on my Top Ten Boldness List, Conrad flicked his indicator and pulled into the No Brussels Sprouts Café.

The No Brussels Sprouts Café's disdain for the diminutive cabbage has nothing to do with the vegetable's disgusting taste or sickening skunk-cabbage odor. Stop by and Barry, the owner, will regale you with the story of his Flemish ex-wife who ran off with a lady skier from Whistler. After your meal, remember, please do not proceed to the Duffey Lake secret motorcycle road! Turn your tails around and head toward Whistler and Vancouver.

"Back again, boys," Barry greeted us. "Care to try our No Sprouts, Just Tons of Butter Croissant?" We ordered two, with extra butter. "Sad news. My ex won the Ski Lottery. Still with us, but so very close."

◆ ◆ ◆

August 17, the GTs stopped at a motorcycle rally in the postcard perfect hot springs, lake-side Village of Nakusp, BC (also a great riding area but not a secret). We said our hellos, talked motorcycles, and listened to rally gossip for an hour.

How to describe a biker rally? As a kid, I was disillusioned with scouting and became a dropout. Helping old ladies across streets, which scouting is very fond of pointing to as its raison d'être, screamed that Baden Powell didn't think things through well. "When I'm an old lady," Marta explained, "I'm sure as hell not going to trust some punk ass boy offering to get me across the street. Especially one wearing a kerchief."

Endlessly preparing for an impractical good deed that will never happen, is an utter waste of time. Same goes for reef knots and don't get me started on semaphore. When is the last time you used a reef knot on your motorcycle? Don't be a luddite, buy those knotless straps. If Baden Powell had owned a motorbike, scouting would be a viable movement today. Motorcycles are much better at moulding young minds than reef knots, Grand Howls, or experimenting with same-sex relationships.

A biker rally is the grown-up version of a Girl Guide or Cub Scout jamboree populated mostly with drop-outs and blacklisted-outs, like me. Just with more beverages, drugs and grownup socializing. Some legitimate badge decorated ex-scouts, converts to motorcycling, attend. You'll find them volunteering to tie reef knots for wayward campers. Good to have capable folk to help the bush league campers out. Did I mention, motorcycling is inclusive? Manufacturers, would you like to donate to Motorcycle Guides and Scouts to help develop our youth? As one of the leaders, I will require one your finest bikes, if I'm able to climb on again. We'll need a bunch of those knotless straps as well.

Veterans of sleeping on rocks and listening to snores, we skipped the experience this time and carried on to the Down and Dirty Motel, further south. Affordable: we each had one of those rooms that make you shudder when you walk across the stained carpet without wearing your Lunar Rover Moonboots.

On the morning of August 18th, 2019, the bikes passed over the Canada - US border. Uneventful since Donald never insisted on erecting a wall, or even a, "Please Keep Off the Border," sign.

We crossed the border multiple times a year and were registered in the Homeland Security Computer, filed under *Jackasses*. You two again? I had unconcealed contraband inside my top case. Why didn't they look? Pull me into the interrogation room and drill me about the illegal half-eaten bag of Canadian cherries I'd forgotten to throw out? When I most needed officialdom, it failed me. They're never *Johnny-on-the-spots*, oblivious to impending tragedy. Exceed the speed limit by 7 mph on the salt flats, out comes their gigantic cloud-based government rule book. Controlled by, you guessed it, those damn political scientists. Forget the ten-rule maximum list policy, bureaucrats use gigantic networked computers to store their regulations, take giga-bites out of our bank accounts and suck joy out the brief amount of time we're blessed with. Increasingly, officers in the Catch the Real Bad Guys division, are being transferred to Risk Management Enforcement. "Less controversy, more revenue, and better performance statistics," Marta explained after she got ticketed on her Guzzi for, "using my noggin."

We arrived in Republic, Washington at midday, an hour and a bit south of the border. It was a scorcher, 90F/32C. Our reservation was in Omak, an hour and a half southwest. From there we would ride over the Cascade Mountains to catch a Washington State ferry back to Vancouver Island. More JOY.

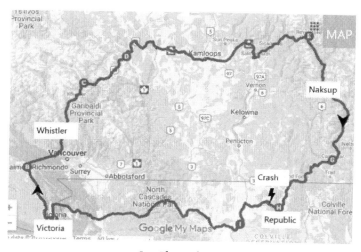

Our Planned Route

HORACE THE HORRIBLE

We pulled the F800s over in the town of Republic to kill time. Ahead of schedule, we didn't want to arrive at our motel prior to the three o'clock check-in. Our leave early stop early rule was problematic. Entirely Conrad's fault. He was leading. Ex-military. Understands the critical nature of time. Logistics expert. Is able to use the twenty-four-clock independent of fingers, toes, ears, and eyes. I'm a Cub Scout flunky for heaven's sake, still focused on considering Marta's snack and washroom maintenance budget request; I can't be watching the clock as well. 'Additional unbudgeted responsibilities." Marta was beginning to sound like a government bureaucrat. Request, denied!

Just after we crossed the border, I asked myself this question: if Steve had included a song in his book, would it be Cyndi Lauper's *Time After Time* or The Chamber Brother's *Time Has Come Today*? I suspect Steve is a secret Brit rocker and the Rolling Stone's *Time Is on My Side* would be up for consideration.

With questions like this to resolve, was I supposed to be paying attention to Greenwich Mean Time and the passage of time as well? I don't even have time to read a *Brief History of Time*. Reader's Digest used to offer classic condensed books for people who shudder at the size of War and Peace. Three hundred pages down to six. *Pegs* wouldn't be a good candidate, but *Zen* and *Time*, maybe. YouTube replaced Readers Digest. Why read six pages when you can watch a two-minute video?

So, there we were, thanks to Conrad, in Republic, ahead of schedule, dressed in full riding regalia, looking forward to tee shirts, shorts, and firing up the motel air conditioner. I was worried; will it be one of those AC units that takes twenty minutes to figure out, another twenty to push out slightly cooler air, all the while sounding like a 737 lifting off, forcing you to switch the damn thing off and have a conniption fit?

Sunday, in the midday heat, not much going on in downtown Republic, Washington. Smart people are at the lake on floaties or sitting in the shade. On August 18th, just Conrad and I parading around the main street in our lunar landing boots and black riding pants, lugging helmets, looking forlorn. I mentioned the clothes were black, right? Black in the heat makes for hot, sweaty, foolish bikers. Several air-conditioned cars passed. Stares through rolled up windows. Having fun boys? What a couple of jackasses! Ever hear of air conditioning?

Desperately we searched for an open, air-conditioned shop. Someone please take us in! For the love of God, rescue us from this blast furnace! Eureka! One coffee-gift shop was open. We ordered lattes and a History of Republic souvenir book. Are you kidding me? We ordered sodas, with extra ice and a Brussels sprout croissant. Kidding again! We ordered eclairs, and were way too hot and bothered to thumb a magazine, let alone a turgid history book without a speck of motorcycle news. Sodas done, we took our time inspecting the gift-ware, enjoying the coolness. We examined the porcelain, made in China, figurines without making a purchase. Same for the Republic, Washington fridge magnets, with one eye alert for the commissioned, salesperson waiting to pounce and give us the hard sell. Prey on our vulnerability. "Your wife would love this one. Don't want to go home empty handed, do you boys?" *No, we'd rather have cheap figurines thrown at us. Got any expensive jewellery or gardening stuff?*

Here's a note to the shop owner: while it's clever entrepreneurship to diversify in small markets, take my advice—dump the marketing consultant's gift-ware idea and add motorcycle accessories. It's rider-country hereabouts, with a popular annual rally site close by. Guaranteed sales when Conrad, I, or the other hundred bikers drop by. Also, tell the *History of Republic* author to include some motorcycle photos! We know Republic enjoys a proud two-wheel history, not stretching back as far as the Moses dirt bike, but noteworthy.

Finally, when we could offer no reasonable explanation for our failure to purchase a figurine, we left the sweet coolness, pulled our jackets on, climbed on our GTs, and headed west on Highway 20 toward Omak. It was around one-thirty. Conrad had us dawdling, trying not to arrive before check-in time. It's cooler in motion, moving along the highway. We connected by intercom for the occasional chit-chat. A distraction? Yes, but also a way to stay alert and share pertinent information. Is that Dicky hiding up ahead? Take immediate evasive action! "Lock on bearing two niner." Conrad would lapse into military jargon. *What the fuck are you talking about, sailor?*

The bikes cruised along on the outskirts of Republic, doing little more than the posted fifty mile an hour limit, passing large hobby farms and pine forest. Not much traffic in either direction. Great visibility and perfect road conditions. MRR low key, no reason to get the drones circling. Visors open, other than the heat, pretty much ideal. Log another safe riding day. A short day. A bit of a being-stubborn-in-a-good-way day. Monday we'd pass through the Cascade mountains and drop to the Pacific Ocean. Motorcycling as it should be.

We were in a wildlife area. Folklore has it that dawn and dusk are prime activity hours. Unlike mad dogs and Englishmen, deer know better than to leap

about in the midday heat. They have their own set
of ten survival rules. Don't Do Something Stupid, includes lying low in blast furnace weather.

Here's a Best Practice Tip for spotting wildlife:

Think like a hunter.

If you're already a hunter, you're home free. If
not, read hunting tips in Field and Stream, watch Al-
aska TV survival shows, and sign up for a gun course.
In a few years you'll be ready to resume motorcycling, unless you've taken up hunting and have run out
of time, in which case read *A Brief History of Time*,
smarten up, and get your priorities straight!

Other than Conrad and his wild turkey, we had
a clean record. When we leave wildlife alone, we expect the same courtesy in return. A peaceful co-ex-
istence. A pact endorsed by PETA without need for
those UN peace keepers who can't actually keep the
peace because, you guessed it, political scientists
call the shots. Conrad and I are naturally respectful
of wildlife, not to the same extent as the Buddha's
list, which includes malaria-infected mosquitoes and
cockroaches, but then we're jackasses, not gods. Our
pets, Pearl and Axel, will (mostly) verify our good
standing, despite the occasional kick in the ribs. I'm
kidding: they never kicked us. They're our ambas-
sadors, spreading the word with their feral friends.
We're so proud, here's a photo:

My dog Pearl and Conrad's Axle

If a troublesome renegade beast were to break our agreement, as expert riders on sophisticated machines, we'd call on our skills, execute an instinctual maneuver, and avoid whatever problem was posed. All angles were covered, except for the scheduling

fiasco, which Conrad was solely responsible for and
working to adjust.

But. You. Just. Never. Can. Tell.

Take Conrad's turkey on the American prairie.
Flat. Open. Uneventful. Not the best place to launch
a sneak attack. But the gobbler did. "Maybe it knew
about the element of surprise," Marta offered? "Strike
when least expected." It was down, flat to the ground
on its belly, waiting to spring. Trained by PETA? Beyond Pearl's and Axel's sphere of influence? Or deaf
to their declaration: "Let them pass! Our masters respect wildlife! They're anti-animal holocaust, but do
enjoy a free-range steak, as do we, now and then."
Pearl and Axel's message is complex.

I had a plan to deal with the worst-case scenarios, should my number come up. A secret weapon,
my old desert riding skills. I'd done some dipsy doodling that street riders never get to do. Using my dirt
bike experience, I'd put my bike into a slide and walk
away with a damaged machine, an insurance claim,
and a few minor bruises. Or attack the obstacle like a
berm and jump over it. Maybe do a 360 before landing? No need to worry when you've studied motorcycle physics. Especially in the scorching midday
heat when animals hunker down under cover knowing the GT guys respect wildlife.

It didn't happen that way. There's always a
smart ass, a renegade. A trouble maker. Flunked out of
cubs. Told to hunker down until it cools, they do the

opposite.

When your number comes up, kryptonite disarms your secret power and shit happens. I don't know how it works, it just does, but it's similar to black hole theory, which is why some consider *Scraping Pegs* and Steve's work to be "companion books." A deli owner goes so far as to suggest *Pegs* should be read first, followed by *A Brief History* to fill in any gaps with what Marta calls, "Pixie dust."

A huge stag, a bit larger than Blue, Paul Bunyan's legendary ox, hid in the pine forest, thinking about sex. Watching the two pretty GT does approach on the road. The first was dark-colored and not really his type, but the second was pure white with a super cute sexy teal accent along her flank. Granted, she was moving faster than the stag normally liked and she had a weird lump sitting on her back, but she would most definitely do.

The stag was on the high side of the road, in a crouch, hidden by the forest. Paul Bunyan was gone, but Deadeye rested there in nonchalant immobility, rifle cocked. The stag calculated speed and distance, ready to spring at precisely the right moment. This doe was his! He had the computation abilities of NASA and impeccable timing, fine-tuned with a power boost dose of deer testosterone. His judge of distance was bang on, and his landing precise.

In the grip of lust, he failed to hear the forest creatures singing Pearl and Axel's message in gentle harmony, "Word is, these two are alright, Horace. Let them pass."

I had no inkling. My radar wasn't focused on impending doom. I was slipping in and out of Motorcycle Paradise. No notion I was in danger of colliding with a buck suffering from heatstroke. In the moments just prior to our encounter, I ruminated that Pink Floyd's *Time* would be another excellent song to include in Steve's book. Will Conrad make the necessary schedule adjustment so I won't have to convince the motel desk clerk that checking out hours early is a fair trade for checking in minutes early? It'll be a great ride through the mountains tomorrow.

Slap–MRR's running fine. Everything under control.

The first I knew of him was seeing a pair of enormous antlers in front of my tiny windscreen. Our eyes locked in a death stare for a split second. MMR said, *oh no Rule #8, might as well pack it up. That's us done for now.*

Rule #8, Your Number May Come Up, trumps what little we know about outsmarting destiny. Doesn't matter that you've been diligently on the lookout, following an ex-military scout, have exceptional skills and a perfect bike, or really understand black holes, when your number comes up, you're getting a prize, like it or not. Had I been one hundred percent focused on renegade wildlife, I still would not have seen Horace the Horrible lurking, targeting my GT, until it was too late to react. Suicidal stealth deer, with cruise missile-like targeting capability, are impossible to defend against. It's like the earth opening up a smidgeon in front of you. It happens *out of the blue.* I can hear Risk Mitigation Guy triumphantly declaring, "Told you so! Should have bought that tank! Oh, no. Don't listen to a risk expert. What do they know?"

Fuck you, Risk Mitigation Guy! Sit in your god damn tank and gloat. At least skiers are uncaged. And the Flemish? Talk about bold risk-taking eaters! I'll take my chances. I'd rather face the consequences than listen to your constant, *the sky is falling rhetoric!*

My stag was more precise than the ten-pound gobbler that launched itself out of a ditch and landed just off target on the right side of Conrad's RT. Had the clandestine animal revenge movement become more sophisticated? Every so often you hear about slaughter animals escaping on their way to the abattoir, not because Forgetful Pants failed to secure the door—no, it's because animals are waking up and fighting back. To them we're Nazis. Who can blame them? We've forced wildlife to declare war on us. Political scientists, stop flipping dead meat and get on this!

Horace the Horrible

Back to Horace... In an instant, his enormous rack of antlers appeared in front of my mini windscreen. It wasn't Christmas eve; unless Rudolph and Santa conduct summer training runs, I knew I was in serious trouble. I saw antlers. Did I tell you they were enormous? As the expression goes, there was *fuck all I could do about it.* Sighting through his high-tech laser scope, DD pulled the trigger. Duck going down! GT knocked to shit. Driver, claim your lotto prize. Death Lottery winner as well?

Bang on target was exactly right. He was on target and we went BANG! I heard the impact; even with earplugs and wearing a helmet, it was deafening. Blasting over the wind and engine noise. That in-the-moment-crushing impact sound can't be described. Yes, it's deafening and terrifying, but it also carries the sound of tragedy and death, like the scream of a bunny being skinned alive. Maybe it's similar to the big bang? The other Steve, Mr. King, probably nailed it in one of his horror stories. Steven King doesn't write academic books, but the sound of my motorcycle colliding with Horace was otherworldly, and that's Mr. King's forte.

I went up and came down. That was it; in the end there wasn't much to tell. Like Mary's accident, summarized in her medical notes as: "She flew over the handlebars and hit her bare head on the pavement when she landed." The rest of the notes are fluff. If they made a Reader's Digest condensed novella about my crash, it would say, "He went up and came down." End of story.

The microsecond before contact, I realized what was about to happen. Like a sped-up version of standing on a ship deck, in shark-infested waters, watching torpedoes lock in. Or being in the Secret Bunker witnessing impending nuclear annihilation on the radar screen. I didn't engage the brake, move to turn the bike, or go into a defensive slide. The expert dipsy doodling maneuvers I carried in my head, the insurance I processed that would get me out of trouble if ever I had to avoid an obstacle quickly, failed to translate to physical action. You can only do so much in an unexpected half-second. No time to save yourself. The Truth About Motorcycling is: you can become as helpless as a baby. No longer an outlaw, superhero, racer, explorer, desert rider or quiet cruiser.

At sixty miles an hour, I rode straight into a three-hundred-pound barrier, putting myself at the mercy of physics, luck, traffic, my riding gear, and my physical capability to withstand Newton's laws of force, the impending collision with the ground. No choice but to be a Guinea pig. Just like Mary, except she had done something stupid, and I had not.

I wonder what the Buddha, resting in the circuitry of my GT according to Mr. Pirsig, thought when we crashed? Must have scared the shit out of

Him. Did my crash cause his Holiness to think differently about universal truths? Or was Robert Pirsig whistling Dixie? I'm not sure. Buddha hitching rides on motorcycles is something I'd like to explore further if I'm not dead or comatose. Maybe I'll use one of those pencils you hold in your mouth and tap out this message: "Conrad, next time you're *on-motorcycle*, please do some pondering on the Buddha-Motorcycle Connection question, instead of constantly monitoring schedule. I suspect it may be a load of crapola."

Or perhaps Buddha wandered into the bush to console Horace during his passage through the Valley of Death? He'd do it for a snake in the grass, so why not a sex crazed stag?

Rule #8, restated with a more fatalistic bent, says:

There are only two kinds of bikers: those that have been down and those that are going to go down.

It's a blessing that there is no time to think when something potentially deadly happens. No moments of panic. No terror. No, *please God, I promise to do better if you rescue me from this unforeseen, shitty, horrific development.* No time to scold yourself for not buying a low mileage used tank. "Dark blue would look nice in the garage. Do you have one with the seat upgrade and an enhanced sound system? So, Bunny and I can relax in it. No second guessing your decision to ride a few more years before hanging up the keys with an unblemished record. Rent a tank RV and visit

the Secret Bunker in Scotland. Thank god I didn't purchase a figurine at the coffee-gift shop. Would have
been in pieces before my wife had a chance to throw it
at me.

When you come to an unexpected, instantaneous stop on a motorcycle, bad things happen. Your
limbs get caught and snap as you're rocketed off the
bike. Your head hasn't even touched down and you're
already fucked-up. Too late to review your protective gear choices. No checking to see if you forgot to
fasten your helmet strap properly or if your boots are
snapped tight.

VALLEY OF DEATH

Horace and I have collided, but I haven't hit the ground yet. While I'm still flying, like a circus clown shot from a cannon without a net to land in, I should tell you another near death story. Again, it's real life, down-to-earth, nonfiction. Not speculative cosmic conjuring, philosophic musings, or outlaw biker fiction.

I almost drowned once. In a river, like Bob. I was meant to be in a canoe, not on a motorcycle. As the expression goes, I really thought it was "tits up" for me. Because I flunked out of Cubs, I'd missed the lesson on shaky watercraft safety which included, don't do something stupid and capsize. Drowning takes time, it's nothing like being shot off a motorcycle into the pavement. They say your life flashes before you when your mind realizes death is imminent. It happened to me when I almost drowned in the Kitimat River. I was ready to let go. Stop struggling. Slip under the water. Pass through the Valley of Death. But fate intervened and dragged me out, one minute before I was to become fish food.

I wonder if Bob got a video? And if he did, was I in it?

I didn't get a replay of the life-flashing-before-my-eyes video when I was flying through the air, nor as I lay on Highway 20. True, I had already seen it once, but there'd been years of living added since my close call. Not even a clip of the new material played. My guess (but this is really Professor Hawking's area, so check his book)—is that there's a time calculation involved. Here's what I think: too fast, like a vehicle accident, no video due to lack of time. Too slow, like dying of cancer or starvation. No video because you have plenty of time to self-review, no need to do all the rush work required to create a nice, life-story recap presentation.

More important than time, in all cases, there can be no doubt the subject is about to enter the Valley of Death. When I almost drowned, I was certain. It wasn't, "I'm scared to death" or "in a life and death struggle." *Yea, though I walk through the Valley of the Shadow of Death; I will fear no Evil.* That's how it was for me in the fast-flowing river, with hypothermia and a belly full of water. I was at peace, done with struggling, ready to let go and pass through the Valley of Death. Into the arms of God and Motorcycle Heaven. It's the only supernatural experience I've had. *Fear no evil.* It's a good one to carry in your back pocket in case you collide with a large animal. The Valley of Death had a profound effect on my development; without it, I'd be a Total Asshole instead of simply just another Jackass. Or perhaps a Political Scientist or Blockhead?

I'm now on the descent leg of the parabolic arc of my post-Horace-encounter, pre-hit-the-road flight. I'm being propelled toward the ground like a stray North Korean test missile. Peace and harmony are not considerations. I'm a renegade projectile at war with the world, with my coconut perfectly positioned to be the first point of contact. The evidence suggests the reality of what happened—first my helmet, then my shoulder took the initial blow. My hip smashed into the ground next. I might have bounced, a raggedy-bone doll skimming like a rock over pavement.

Flesh and blood versus asphalt. It's not a fair fight. Not a thing you can do about it. You can be stubborn in a good way all you like, but what's the point? You've won the lottery:

The Jig's Up, You Move from Motorcycle Riding Rules to God's Rules.

FEAR NO EVIL

I t all happened in the time it takes to change the TV channel. No mortal could comprehend the reality of how that second of time split neatly down the middle—the first half second was incomprehensible; the other half second began the journey of human tumbleweed.

Flying blind, lost in the Secret Bunker of my mind, not focused on the inescapable big bang ahead of me. The great news is you can just be there, in the moment, already with broken bones, not worried about the stopping part. No need to question: will I live or die? Or walk again? Drool like a bloodhound waiting for food, forevermore? No thoughts of how dressing in haute couture will work with those bags you have to pee into. You won't even have time to think about how you'll never have to worry about shitting your pants again—because your plumbing's out of order. Just cobwebs growing down there.

So, if you're ever in this unfortunate situation, here's the best tip I've got:

Enjoy your time in the air. It's not going to get bet-ter.

Afterwards, when the rocket flight is over, and the capsule has crash-landed on the surface of the road, this will scream inside your head: *this is about to hurt like hell, isn't it?* Take a brief inventory of body parts and you'll actually be thinking *nope, not like hell, it's* way *worse.* If you're even thinking then. Maybe Helmetless Mary McGregor was lucky?

In Bill Bryson's book "Down Under" he recounts the story of a man stung by a box jellyfish (Marta confused them with eels. "I know motorcycles, not fish," she explained), widely thought of as having the most painful sting of all forms of wildlife on a human (hate to have one of those stuck in my helmet—bees are bad enough)!   In his story, when the man is stung, he begins to scream louder than virtually any man in history. Paramedics come and sedate him and take him off to hospital. Here's the kicker: even sedated. He was still screaming.

So maybe the next tip should be:

If you're lying on the road screaming, think of that guy on an Aussie beach and count your lucky stars that box jellyfish prefer water.

Bill's Nameless Screamer probably never rode a motorcycle, so naturally he was upset. If you're fired off a bike thanks to wildlife, you'll think, *at least I got a ride in beforehand.* Poor Screamer was wading in shallow water, killing time, when wildlife attacked him. No wonder he screamed blue murder. No motorcycle preJOY!

Presently, I'm lying face up in the middle of the road, the hot orange-yellow August sun frying me like meat under the broiler at Tony's deli. A relentless sun, like being on an Aussie beach, except bordered by a green pine forest instead of blue waves and jelly-fish. A beautiful day for Horace the Horrible to die a miserable death. I have no recollection of bones snap-ping, of going over the bars and sailing through the air before the asphalt, ever so efficiently, broke my fall, my body absorbing the impact energy in accordance with Newtonian law.

My mind ducked down and covered itself with a warm baby blanket. You'd think it would be in a frenzy, filing reports, testing limbs, and having a ser-ious conversation with God, but it didn't have a clue; it was empty, like a political scientist looking at a math test.

Left Brain and Right Brain were chatting:

"Duck and cover, under that blanket."

"Save ourselves," said Left.

Right, ever the child followed readily, agreeing, "There's nothing we can do! We'll check in later, if we're still ticking."

"I don't think we're dead," Left reassured Right.

"Not just yet anyway."

Right peeked out from under the mental safety blanket and saw both bike and body wrecked. Conrad was swinging his machine around, horrified.

"We're deep in the brown smelly stuff, that's for sure. Luckily, no box jellyfish in sight."

With that, my mind shut down as MRR reached over and tapped *Fear No Evil* in my back pocket. *You take it from here, Fear. Who knows if I'll be back? Doesn't look good.*

One minute *on-bike*, a little bored and hot. Now *off-bike*, in shock, both sides of my brain in protective shutdown mode. No part of my body trying to move; I felt no urgency to do anything other than lie back and accept the consequences of my motorcycle choice. *Why didn't I choose tank?* If the friends of Horace had dispatched an army of spiders, snakes, and jellyfish on a revenge mission, I wouldn't have cared. How much worse can it get?

At some point my brain popped up again, on minimal cycles. Slowly, like an old computer running a glitchy operating system. It wondered about the body, the way one thinks about the outcome of a football game or the new menu item at the No Brussels Sprouts Café or what Tony's up to with the Cosmic Special. As the captain of my ship, I needed a damage assessment:

Seal off bulkhead compartment three!

It's beyond hope, Captain!
We're going down if it can't be repaired! Come on.
You must take charge!

Nerves reported back. Our ship's not intact Captain. We may go down. Unorthodox body behaviours observed, but no white-hot daggers like Lenny described. Sometimes it's best to leave well enough alone and not go looking for trouble. Allow your mind to cower under the blanket a while longer. *What can I do? Bulkhead compartment three will have to seal itself. I'm not afraid to walk in the Valley of Death. Lying on the pavement in the scorching sun isn't as peaceful as drowning in a river, but it's not that bad. At least it's warmer.*

This isn't a tip, it's John Prine logic:

When the shit hits the fan, you must play the cards you're dealt. It is what it is, and it ain't what it ain't.

Right Brain looked at its cards, thought, *Left can handle this*, and out of respect for the little it knew about survival techniques elected to fold. Unable to cope in a situation too esoteric for most, the overwhelmed grey matter threw in its hand and yelled, "Pass," leaving Left alone to run the ship. Thanks to Left, I remained calm. No hysterics or sense of urgency. *Just lie here like a deflated blow-up doll and wait. Let me figure something out. No promises! I've not dealt with this before and the rest of our body has abandoned us.*

There was nothing to do but lie still. "No sense getting bent out of shape," Left said calmly, with a light chuckle at the irony. "A semi may run us over, but, hey ho, that's life and death for us at this point. At least we died tryin'. Always suspected we should have gone with the tank option."

Right would have been out of control: *A semi! Move! Move! Get up! You're going to die and then what'll I do? Rot six feet under? Any idea how ineffective rotten brain matter is?* Right can be such a drama queen.

Doctors say there is a release of endorphins and adrenaline to increase physical alertness and elevate mood, making it easier to handle a crash. The hormones block pain and the stress to keep you calm. I must have had a ton of anti-anxiety hormones circulating; enough to allow me to relax in the middle of the highway, in the scorching heat, content to let fate unfold. There was an acceptance, like being in the Kitimat River on the edge of death, except I expected I'd soon be up duct taping GT back together.

The pain wasn't like a Charlie-horse, sudden and severe. It seeped slowly into my nothingness. "Remain perfectly still and the pain will fade," my brain ordered. "Rest awhile, then we'll try organizing our parts, to move. Maybe even stand up."

Moving would surely please Conrad, who now stood over me, looking distressed and probably thinking: *Will I have to spoon feed him soup when I visit from now on? Shove those soft jelly candies he detests through his dribbling gums? Maybe sneak in a Brussels sprout as a joke? Ha ha, that would be funny. Bet he'll make the most disgusting gurgling noises when we go out for coffee. How long till I can stop dropping by?* These are obvious thoughts when you come across a person jettisoned off of a motorcycle, and that person is your friend.

When you come across a stranger slung off of a motorcycle, you may be considerably less kind. *Probably did something stupid. What a Blockhead! Thanks for screwing up our schedule with the road closure, dickhead!*

In my shock induced trance, I stood unaided and imagined strangers circled around me, applauding, "He's up. With all that gear on. Dodged a bullet! What a great attitude! Look at the size of those boots! Could have been worse, that's for sure." And I'd say to Conrad, *Everything's all right, buddy. Just a bump—give me a moment or two to compose myself and we'll be on our way. You can MacGyver my GT together, right? You're good at sorting things out. What's that? You'll organize a search and destroy mission for Horace?"*

But all I could do was lie in a calm daze, Fearing No Evil. I couldn't speak. My brain vaguely thinking: *Should have taken more time to say goodbye when I left home.* Conrad spoke, but I couldn't make out what he was saying. *What's that you saying, Conrad?* I asked (if 'asking' really means 'staring blankly'). Conrad repeated his question, given my lack of response —could I move off the center line toward the side of the road? I almost died laughing (if 'laughing' really means 'staring blankly').

Sensible idea though, Left said after analyzing the situation. *Not getting run over is a sound course of action. Let's work on it, work it... Get our parts moving now.* The left side of my body, from the shoulder down, was inoperable, dead weight. Broken, fractured, inflamed, bruised, and leaking. At the time, I assumed it just needed more time to recover. The absence of massive mind-numbing pain signals meant my body would be responsive soon. Waiting might result in parts of me coating a massive truck tire, so I reached way down and had my right leg push me over an inch. Couldn't manage more. "That inch will have to do," Left muttered. "All we got, I'm afraid."

Thankfully, vehicles had stopped, and the road was soon blocked, so not even that inch was necessary. Bystanders were horrified (except a delighted, show-me-the-blood type, lad). Lying flat on my back, like a corpse, it was impossible to observe what was going on, but I was vaguely aware of commotion as I was reinforced the foolishness of motorcycle riding. One of the congregated turned out to be an Emergency Medical Technician, and yet another was a nurse. How lucky is that? What are those odds? My number came up, but part of this prize was somebody useful to deliver it to me. Yahoo Buddha! Way to go! Have you abandoned GT to direct recovery operations? Thanks for squeezing out of the circuitry to help out! The truth is: I'm glad Buddha is a motorcyclist.

Poor jellyfish screamer, lying on that Australian beach, didn't have motorcycle accommodations, so no Buddha. Just a couple of partying drunk welders from New South Wales until the paramedics showed up. Understand why he was screaming his bloody head off? What about Bob? Is Buddha a good swimmer? How did He get out of the Thompson River and why didn't he take Bob with Him?

The EMT took charge. I didn't have to do a thing; I was in the hands of Super Samaritan. He issued instructions, established control. Impressed the hell out of Left Brain. He also positioned two ladies in front of me to act as a sunscreen. What a guy; what an outstanding job! I looked at the two new arrivals, unable to say *thank you, ladies. I'm sure this isn't what you had planned for your Sunday afternoon outing. Stopping in this blazing heat for sun blocker duty?* They smiled down at me, without complaint, and did an outstanding job also–both were stout, robust women: I suppose that's why Super Samaritan selected them. One reminded me of my Auntie Minnie.

"Do not move your head!" *Okay, I'm fine with that for now. I won't argue about whether I have the right to do what ever I choose to do with my own head. Not the best time to drag out my debating skills.* Better to remain a pleasant cooperative blob. Super Samaritan preformed medical checks. Questions were asked. In good hands, I was told. "Lie still. Do not move! Remain conscious and wait for the ambulance to arrive. Who's the dumbass now? Like I was going anywhere soon. *Okay, no problem.* I used facial expressions to pass information along and uttered childlike sounds. *No need to make a fuss. Give me a minute. I'll get up and be on my way soon. You're all excellent people, but it's too much. Unnecessary. Really. Just give me a few minutes. Wait... Did you say ambulance?*

I didn't recall ordering an ambulance.

"You'll be all right. I'm going to dribble some water into your mouth now." Super Samaritan assured me. "Relax." I did a good job relaxing and even managed a few swallows of the cool liquid with my helmet on and visor up. Half of it ran down my chin. Let the drooling commence! *Yes, I know I'll be all right,* I wanted to answer, *after all, I almost drowned once. I understand what it's like to drift toward the Valley of Death. This isn't it. I'm fine. Let me sleep. Thanks for your concern. You're extremely nice, folks, and damn fine sun blockers!*

People carried on one-sided conversations with me to keep me alert. I wondered if the good Samaritans appreciated my *Fear No Evil* demeanor? No hollering blue murder and carrying on like the Screamer with the teeny weenie jellyfish sting. Australians can be so over-the-top.

A state trooper attended the accident scene. I saw his enormous hat pointed down at me. It did a good job blocking the sun from his face, like the two ladies standing over me. Conrad told him about the deer. The cop seemed suspicious; *it's always a deer.* Never, *truth be told, he was behaving like a Blockhead, officer.* "Don't worry about your bike." Conrad told me. He would collect what I needed, especially the emergency travel insurance document in the top box. He'd look after GT. They wandered off to inspect the evidence.

Lots of sirens. Each one with a unique sound. The state trooper's first. Then a fire truck, followed shortly by the ambulance. It wasn't low key. A real hullaballoo. Motorcycle accident! One victim. Logged into the system. Full response code red! Sirens wailing. Lights flashing. Hospital Emergency ready for incoming. Futile to resist. No chance of doing a low-key duct tape, zap strap, repair and carry-on job now. "You'll be all right," Super Samaritan kept reminding me. It was unnerving. *Why would I not be alright?*

From the recently arrived ambulance came an on-duty EMT who carefully replaced my helmet with a neck brace. Head was locked in, unable to move. My riding pants had zippers up the legs — my pants came off. The EMT explained that they cut most rid-

ing pants off. I smiled. Yes, my lucky day! I'll be need-
ing those pants to ride home soon.

In a professional drill that involved counting to
three (which I was able to follow to anticipate lift-
off), they hoisted my body up and onto a stretcher. I
was very impressed. First class, not like some hunter
found me and dragged my ass into the back of their
old pickup beside a moose carcass.

They placed me in the ambulance, covered
with a thin blanket, hooked up to an IV drip, and gave
me some pills. No one asked if I wanted a ride. Maybe I
prefer to hitch hike? Or stay put and get a lift from one
of the sun-blocker ladies if need be? When you're in an
accident, things happen to you; you don't have a say.
You're like beef on route to a processing plant, except
with the opposite intent. The siren wailed and off
we went, headed east, back the way we came, toward
the coffee-gift shop. My first ambulance ride. GT was
abandoned, crippled and alone. Conrad will sort her
out, I prayed. *Poor thing.*

In the Kitimat River drowning, it had been
quiet. Peaceful and serene. It's a nice way to go. No
one fussed over me. Into the world alone. Out of the
world alone, but not feeling alone: Fear no Evil accompanied me. It was nothing like having a motorcycle accident on an American highway. It's a great
big hullaballoo.

It's impressive, how organized rescue and repair processes snatch bodies off public infrastructure

and take them in for repair. Their routines are devoid of indecision. If you're the body, you'll be part
of a military-like operation staffed by friendly angels
of mercy. Wonder if they ever get pissed off? Have
bad days? Thanks a lot, asshole! I was in the middle
of binging Breaking Bad and heating nachos. Not in a
mood to be comforting, but you'll still be getting our
HUMONGOUS BILL!

     Left whispered, "What's that? A big bill?"
     "I'll have to pay for all this?"
     "We're not in the land of socialized medicine;
they don't roll fire trucks for free here."
    "I'll be charged for the fire truck? Nothing's on
fire! Never ordered any of this. I'll be charged even
though I didn't place an order?"
    "Yup, you will" Left said. Matter of factly. "Costs
are heading toward the stratosphere and we have
no say. Too bad you didn't read your el cheapo insurance policy."

    Right popped up from nowhere and rattled on
hysterically, repeating the financial-medical horror
stories we had taken in over the years. I visualized
the billing meter going round and round, like carnival
ducks, picking up speed with every revolution and
siren blare. The billing scenario unfolding like leaving your bike at No Discussion Motorcycle Service.
A mechanic pushes it to the back and starts fiddling
without saying a word. "Here's your big bill, buddy!
It lists out everything we did, including all the unnecessary stuff you never asked us to do." You spot

the $137.50 per screw item. "You can't be too careful. Can you sell your house and car? If need be, we can put in nonOEM screws for a little less, next time, when you've moved into your moldy rat-infested trailer."

Then it was official—my record was entered in the medical billing system under Motorcycle Jackass with El Cheapo Insurance. I was along for the expensive ride, dealt with by very nice, attentive, highly skilled, caring people. The best people. Well balanced brains. Much better than bouncing along in the back of a hippie pickup truck with a washed-up ex-political scientist.

Here's my final tip for now:

Always be nice to Buddha. You may need all the help you can get one day.

PART 6 – WELCOME TO BLOBLAND

FERRY MEMORIAL

Ferry County Memorial Hospital in Republic, Washington, established 1945, is surrounded by great motorcycle roads and staffed by the finest angels of mercy. The hospital doesn't promote the motorcycle roads (although they're not as secret as the Duffey Lake Road: remember, not a word) despite the significant revenue that flows into the hospital coffers from the rivers of damaged bikers that stream through its doors. Make a note-to-self, Mr. Republic Shop Owner with air-conditioning and figurines for sale, look to the local hospital for business strategies.

Hospitals around the globe are at the forefront of the motorcyclist repair business. Can't be repaired? They have morgues, of course—though there's less money in dead people. And less looking after—unless you call adjusting the freezer temperature good hospitality.

There are a few Motorcycle State of Mind riders whose numbers come up, but Ferry Memorial mostly attends to clueless weekend warriors and SQUIDS.

You don't know what a SQUID is? It's definitely a case of you know-one-when-you-see-one. Nonetheless, I turned to the Urban Dictionary to get you a better definition:

> *A young motorcyclist who overestimates his abilities boasts of his riding skills when in reality he has none. SQUID bikes are usually decorated with chrome and various anodized bits. Rear tires are too wide for their own good, swingarm extended. Really slow in the corners, and sudden bursts of acceleration when a straight appears. SQUIDs wear no protection, deeming themselves invincible. This fact compounds itself with the fact that they engage in 'extreme riding,' performing wheelies and stoppies in public areas. SQUIDs wreck a lot. A contraction of the phrase 'squirrely kid'.*

Now you know the Urban Dictionary definition. Maybe a bit harsh? Start out of sight in a desert to skip being a SQUID.

Difficult, though, even for experienced hospital staff to tell the Blockheads from the SQUIDs from the experts—they all look alike on stretchers, pant-less, wearing neck braces. They're all more incoming from the, "impact injury generators."

Everyone likes to put their best foot forward. Make a good impression. On the day they wheeled in me, how did they size me up? I'll never know, but I'll always wonder. Obviously, they process many downed ducks because I kept hearing, "You're not our first one…" It's a stock phrase, repeated to make the incoming feel better. Thank god, I thought! *They're experienced. They know how to repair motorcyclists. It's okay that I'm pant-less and vulnerable, like when I was two years old.*

Tough guy and gal bikers aren't so carefree and bold when they're wheeled in scared half to death. Their joyous, the world is my oyster, outlaw ride of Zen-like self-discovery, one with the Earth, brought to a crashing halt by an attempt to be at one with the Earth. I was in the group that avoided the black guide line on the hospital floor — "Follow Black to the Morgue"—and then, "Welcome to Our Morgue," instead I rode the red line to the ER. *Is that a painted line, or is it my blood trail dripping off the gurney?* The ride to ER is much shorter than the trip to the morgue, which is downstairs, at the end of the hall, next to the boiler room. ER is always beside Admin, where they prepare your humongous bill.

Riders never foresee their adventures ending in the ER. It's always a shock despite this certainty: it's a matter of when, not if.

They take confidence in whatever track or dirt ribbons they've won, or the strength of their Iron Butt credentials, but it all counts for diddly squat on an Emergency Room gurney. "Thought it would never happen to me," their terrified expressions tell the angels of mercy. The nurses know better. "Believe me, honey, you're not the first one who thought that. Yet, here you are. Strange how that works, huh? So predictable." They frown at Risk Management Guy. Tanks aren't good for business.

Hospitals are intimidating when you're not familiar with their mysterious ways and are lying in a supine position, without pants, in a head restraint, and pumped full of drugs. Which are needed because the emergency examination beds are about as comfortable as that hot highway pavement, regardless of how injured you might be. The nurses were friendly as they performed the requisite medical checks—it was like having my mom, aunts, and sisters all there; just before obligatory kindergarten nap time. The left side of my brain hadn't yet come up with a plan beyond, *wait it out. Soon they'll be done. One step at a time. Slap on a couple of Band Aids. Eventually they'll let us move, swivel Head around and rise from the examination table like the second coming of Christ (maybe a tad overstated. More like - move Head thirty degrees to each side and creak forward while holding flimsy hospital dress down). Wait for Conrad to sort things out.* The process can't be rushed.

A giant needle appeared, wheeled in by a smiling, gentle-faced nurse. I hate needles. When I was young, I struggled to remain upright at the sight of a needle or a drop of blood. Age has hardened me; now I merely tremble. The nurse now looked like the psycho who tortures an author in Steven King's *Misery. Kathy Bates is working at Ferry Memorial?* Now, I was shaking. "Just an Aspirin please and I'll be on my way," Left suggested. "When you come out of shock, you'll need it," the nurse told me, waving her humongous spike at me. "You're not my first. Believe me." I didn't believe her and almost asked to see her qualifications before she could skewer me. *Are you certified to use that thing? Did you attend the Humongous Needles, a Gentler Approach seminar last month? Or you're old school? Step forward. Thrust. Reload.*

Then I asked myself, who am I, a former fainter, to question medical experts? *They know the drill. It's not new to them. Would I tell Valentino Rossi how to take a corner? No! Question Professor Hawking's decisions if we were floating around the Cosmos together? No! No! No! Second guess my motorcycle mechanic with all their diplomas on the wall, including "Secret Specialty Tool Certification?" No!*

I could imagine what the rescuers would think: *Listen to this impact inquiry, idiot! After all, we've done for him, sirens, first ride in an ambulance, saving his life, not cutting his pants, even sent the fire truck, he's asking to see our certificates? How dare he? I'm not just going to jab him; I'm going to stab him. Might even use the unnecessarily larger needle. Shut the fuck up! Asshole! Why are you trembling?*

The thought of upsetting the staff scared me even more than the humongous needle. Experience had taught me—you must not offend your bike mechanic. It's not appropriate to question the authorities, local by-laws, or motel front desk staff. I didn't want to come across as a hospital SQUID. I accepted the stabbing and in truth, I'm glad I did. Seems my angels knew what they were doing and were doing one hell of a job. Drugs have a way of changing your perspective and hospitals have wonderful drugs. The best ones come in very large needles.

Time passed; the doctor, "Is on his way." The nursing staff didn't allow movement. Luckily, I had stopped trembling. I was literally stiff as a board and concerned the doc would be less than pleased about being called out on a Sunday to repair another selfish joy rider. *Do you outlaws have absolutely no consideration for others? Good business, but doctors need days off too, you know?*

One of the nurses was from BC. She has relatives in Victoria which makes us practically family. Married an American and the couple visits Vancouver Island frequently. It's weird: if you're damaged or in dire straits and a way from home, meeting a person from your country, region, or village instantly cements a bond. A total stranger, based purely on geography, will bend over backward to help you. Location supercharges an inherent natural desire to assist. BC nurse looked at me, I'm here for you. With Conrad, we were a geographically bonded trio.

Is there a hospital version of dash and dine, I wondered? I couldn't rely on Gigantic Insurance Company to spring me. Everyone's heard insurance company horror stories; desperate policy holders' abandonment in their hour of need. Other than one minor fender bender, I had zero experience dealing with insurers. I'd heard plenty of *the devil is an insurance adjuster* stories though. They're way more bad ass than motorcycle outlaws.

Once the doc looks me over, I'll be declared fit as a fiddle, I deluded myself. An older, well used fiddle, for sure, and somewhat knocked around, out of tune, and scraped up. But capable of making music; Ferry Memorial's obligations will be satisfied. *He can play, Twinkle Twinkle. OK good to go. Can't hold him any longer.*

I debated, is the motorcycle hospital phone call home necessary? Needlessly worry family? Send them off in a tizzy. Am I capable of sorting this out? *After all, I put myself in Ferry Memorial, shouldn't I get myself out? It's not like anyone forced me to ride motorcycles. Buckle down and take care of business. Absolutely no foofaraw! Soreness passes with time. Conrad knows how to sort things out. Make use of his military training. Flee the battle zone!*

The emergency doctor, a young man, arrived for the examination. He was very professional. Left and Right muttered quietly to each other, impressed, and a little intimidated. At his side, an x-ray technician waited his turn; the tech mentioned that he had been called in on his day off, though didn't seem upset about it: "Not the first time." he said. I wondered if he did piece work? Per motorcyclist? Is that the way private medicine works?

In response to the doctor's questions, I mentally uttered some coherent words and told him my version. "It was a close call. I'm battered but intact and ready to get back out there. Duct tape me up, throw on one of those white cloth bandage wraps, perhaps one around my head for dramatic effect, and I'm good to go. Could you spare a few zap straps for GT? I'll pay for them, of course. Add them to my bill. Maybe Gigantic Insurance Company won't notice. I'll make it home just fine." Truthfully, though, all I said was "Hi, Doc." Even that was more whisper than discernible. I wondered; how much does Ferry Memorial charge for a tie strap?

"Hi back at ya," he replied. "I see you've had quite the accident. Totalled your motorbike? I hear you killed Blue? You're not the first impact injury we've seen here, but I can't remember anyone killing Blue before."

Hospital humor? Too far west for Paul Bunyan's big ox. "Stag." I whispered. "Quite a bit larger than Blue." I thought about playing along with the humor. *Did anyone see Buddha wandering around the forest? He's a hefty fellow—easy to spot.* But what if one of the staff is a devout Buddhist? Or reverent of all religions? Not the best time to offend. Turn a nurse into Misery's Kathy Bates. Damn godless heathen! Strap him to the slab! Down the black line. Shove him in the boiler room. He'll be ready for a freezer drawer soon.

No one would get my joke. Not even BC nurse. It'd fall flat on the emergency room floor. Dead. Only Marta would get it, and she wasn't at Ferry Memorial. I'd try to explain, give up, and shrug, "Read Zen and the Art of Motorcycle Maintenance."

"Yes, very sad indeed," the doctor said, mishearing.

"Stag!" I croaked again.

"Yes, it was sad." Now he was looking at me like I was a repetitive idiot. So, I gave up.

A few preliminaries later, the physical exam began.

"Wiggle your toes, please," instructed the doc.

No problemo. Child's play. It elated me. Start with Toes. Is it because they are furthest from Head? A medical diagnostic hard rule? I have full confidence in my toes. I don't know if it was the drugs, or just the fact that I've never had a toe problem, other than a few stubs, and my digits always bounced right back, but I was super confident I could put my toes up against any. Maybe not high wire tight-rope walkers like the Flying Wallendas, but any toes in Emergency on that Sunday.

Who do you love? Drugs. I understand.

I passed Toes with flying colors. Aced it, as they

say.

"Finger movement?"

I wasn't as finger confident. My left shoulder was locked, but I could force my elbow to bend slightly. I twitched my left fingers a bit and finished with a flourish of movement using my right hand.

Good enough? I wanted to put on a show for the nice doctor. *At least there's movement. Not like Toes, but Fingers work. I'm no doctor, but even I can see, they just need rest.*

My eyes followed his finger as requested. At least I thought so. It's much harder to tell with Eyes than with Toes or Fingers. I didn't really have a clue, and the doctor wasn't about to provide an opinion. The legalities of the trade and American litigation kept him zipped up. He nodded occasionally and didn't act horrified; both good signs. *See? All this medical hullaballoo, totally unnecessary. I should clear out, make way for an actual impact injury emergency. I'm sure a SQUID will be along shortly.*

Then the big test. Carefully, my neck brace came off. The doctor's fingers poked around the base of my skull. I could move Head on command. *Hallelujah! Toes, Fingers, Eyes and now Head. All fine. It's a wrap.*

"Ok?" I asked. "I can go?"

The doctor wore his not-so-fast-buster expression and spoke using language he thought I would probably understand, "Just because the wheels turn on a motorcycle, doesn't mean to say it's driveable. At Ferry, we need to check you're ok, so diagnostic investigations are mandatory. I'm your mechanic, so to speak. Robert," he said, gesticulating to the technician, "Will make sure none of your forks are broken, and check for hairline cracks in your handlebars." That's what I heard, while the doc rolled out his medical school terminology on me. I didn't catch any of the terrifying words like, "paralyzed," "spine," or "Mary McGregor," so I relaxed. More waiting. Just like at Service. It's always takes longer than you think.

Robert grabbed the end of the gurney and we headed off to take pictures, following the blue line. More than a dozen shots taken up and down my left side. "We'll do a CAT scan on Monday," the technician said, "You're not the first one we've had, so we know to look out for bleeds on the brain and other stuff you wouldn't understand. Doctor's orders. You'll be transferred to regional for an MRI."

I wasn't listening. I waited, biding my time because that's what you do in Service. Keep your mouth shut and wait. No toe X-rays, I wanted to ask? *They were also in the accident. Yes, I was wearing my lunar rover boots but also a helmet, and you want to check my brain? Seems a bit selective, don't you think? More money in brains than toes? Any idea what a hospital zap strap is worth? I'll need a few to get GT back on the road.*

Robert mentioned the word "MRI," again. And

"ambulance ride Monday to the regional hospital." Not that I won't enjoy another ambulance ride on drugs, but the medical process was spinning out of control. Becoming ridiculous. Billing horror stories were unfolding and panicking me. *It's all true, and it's happening to me! This is exactly how they do it. With drugs and scare tactics. Must accelerate my escape plan!* I hadn't lost an arm and a leg in the accident, but I was about to with the hospital bill. I didn't tell him, "Won't be here Monday. Will have legged it by then. Still have a good one, you know. One ambulance ride is plenty, thanks. Can't afford two. I'm saving for a new motorcycle, you know? Your hospitality's been terrific, but the fire truck was a bit much. And now an MRI? I imagined a huge dollar meter by the door ticking up the bill relentlessly, indefatigably. And what about poor GT? Waiting for me. Alone and forsaken in a strange yard, wondering, does he care? Waiting for me to show up with a few zap straps and nurse her home. Out of reach of the scrap yard. Perform reconstructive surgery. After all, we've been through together. GT never let me down. Not once! Now, a piece of junk?

We headed back to the ER. "I'm not allowed to interpret them," Robert had said when asked about the results. *What the hell do they teach them for two years—how to push a button?* My attention returned to the present: *fine, I can wait for the doctor. Of course, you have your hands full, taking good pictures.* I'm over-reacting, but Robert, you don't have to worry about being bankrupted by the system, I silently lectured the X-ray technician. *Medical boundaries and safeguards are important. Division of duties. I know that. I'm okay with waiting to hear the good news from the nice doctor.*

THE MOTORCYCLE
HOSPITAL CALL

I rested in a dimly lit room, my left leg raised on a pad, my joints on ice, my mind in Blobland, capable of mellow fretting but no anxiety. Conrad was off scouting transportation and accommodation options. "Undrivable," he'd reported back on GT's condition. Nurses dropped in to check on their impact injury. Yes, I'm still here, on ice. You're all so very nice. Like my moms did when I was three (yes, I had more than one mom; I'll explain soon). It's very reassuring knowing angels are just outside the door, not hovering above the bed, waiting to give you the tour. Here's what's on the far side of the Valley of Death. First, the Big Guy would like a word.

"The doctor will return, soon."

BC Nurse located my phone, intact and operational. She slid a second pillow under Head and Shoulders. I picked up my left arm (which had become incapable of movement) with my right hand and swung it over to the phone lying on my chest.

Left fingers gripped the phone in the ready-for-action position. *Now what?* Reluctantly, my brain had accepted the fact, I must make the call. I would not arrive home on schedule and it would be obvious: *things are not as they were when you left. What have you been up to? Ever hear of communication? The thing that rings?*

But what to say? "Hey, my number finally came up! But splendid news! Hardly a scratch!" I felt guilty. Like an alcoholic who falls off the wagon and calls home, "I'm drunk and disgusting. Come and fetch me! Bail me out."

You did it to yourself, buster! What the hell is wrong with you?

Do I think only of myself when I climb on? Why do I gamble and force others to deal with the consequences? No one forced me to buy motorcycles.

The Truth About Motorcycles is: they are very selfish.

When you purchase a bike, your family waits for the call. They know it will come. It's inevitable. Like buying a time bomb with a random counter. Families accept the truth about motorcycles, riders ignore it. They haul out the tired phrase again: "It's not motorcycles, it's the idiots behind the wheels. I'll be fine." Most riders think they're too aware and nimble to have an accident. Not families. They know better.

I rode for years without making the Hospital Call. Not even the Slightly Bruised or Having Mechanical Issues call. It seemed like I might get away Scot-free. It's not impossible.

I must use the thing that rings. Break the news. I rehearsed: be released soon. Just waiting for the doc. Yes, a day or two late. Rule #8, but a very lucky break. I'm right as rain. Fit as a fiddle. You know me, one of the lucky ones.

There is no easy way to begin a conversation that includes, "hospital," and "motorcycle." My wife is emotional, not a stone-cold semi-Newtonian, like me. Accident conversations are simple with left brains. "Not surprised. It was just a matter of time after you bought that thing. Inevitable. What else is new? Anything unusual or out of the norm?"

I decided to text my daughter, a young nurse, a medical professional. The word, "hospital," would not freak her out, she worked at one. We text regularly, nothing unusual about receiving a message from dad. "You there?"

She was. I used the words: hospital, deer, and motorcycle. Most importantly, "I'm fine" and "Conrad." Monica used, "OMG," repeatedly. I suggested she break the news to Mom, on account of her freaking out. I would standby to phone once I got the thumbs up. Monica didn't fall for my ploy. "No way. You need to talk to her yourself. Kids are so much easier when they're young and ignorant and think you're godlike.

It went better than expected. Conditioned by years of waiting for the bad news Hospital Call and, "I'm fine. Yes, I'm in a hospital, but it's not a big deal. A formality, really. You know how these things work? A scratch in a road accident and they haul your ass to the hospital. Can't be avoided. I'll be out soon. Yes, I bought travel insurance. Yes, Conrad is here. Other than the schedule getting screwed up, everything's hunky dory. Right as rain. Couldn't be better. Fit as a fiddle."

We didn't get into insurance details, no revealing my doubts about opting for the *el cheapo* policy option. It was immaterial, given I was fine and would be released before long. It was a colossal relief, getting the Hospital Call off my to-do list. Next, escape and rescue GT. Haul her home in a rental truck.

I have two sisters and three brothers. I'm the youngest. The baby. I'm used to being coddled. I wondered: did Buddha fill Mom and Dad in? The reincarnated version of Mom and Dad?

We have a messaging group, Sibs Gang. I snapped a picture of my toes poking out from under the hospital sheet. "Guess where I am?" That kicked off a flurry of activity. Poor baby! Everyone on standby! Battle stations! Lower the life raft! It's great having two bonus moms and three older brother-protectors.

I also sent the toe picture to the Copley Park Dog Moms. I'm proud to be an Honorary Dog Mom, thanks to Pearl. That triggered another burst of empathy. Ladies with dogs know how to lay it on thick. I felt the opposite of forsaken.

◆ ◆ ◆

There's activity in Emergency. They have switched the lights to stark-sterile-hospital-glare mode. "Doctor is on his way," I was told. The ice packs gone, they prepped me to make my second major medical move of the day. The first being Highway 20-to-gurney-to-hospital examination slab. Other than being there, well... I was just there, like a sack of dead box jellyfish. But move two would be all me. BC Nurse was my instructor for my bed-to-wheelchair attempt. Very promising, I thought. No bad news, and it's common knowledge they show patients the hospital exit door in wheelchairs. No walking out! If you're alive, wheelchair. Deceased, gurney — follow the black line and make a right when you see the, "Welcome to Our Morgue" sign.

My move was to be: Pivot Transfer, Unassisted in the Standing Position. Forget the assisted and squat position transfer movements, they're for patients with real impact injury limitations. Not me. I would only have to master the standing pivot before being wheeled out the exit door. Looked easy. Stand on operational right leg, support myself from the edge of the bed if necessary, pivot and lower into the locked wheelchair. Rear end touchdown must be precise. Don't over shoot! Always double check to ensure the wheelchair is locked! As a precaution, an orderly held the chair. *I ride a motorcycle, remember? Let's get on with it!* I waited patiently, sitting on the edge of the bed in my hospital gown. Kept my mouth shut. *The door is just down the corridor. Don't blow this now with inappropriate remarks! This is the last mandatory procedure.*

"Absolutely no weight on your left leg!"

No problemo. I'm a former three-legged race winner. Grade five, I think it was? This will be a piece of cake. The moment weight transferred to my right leg, and I pushed off the bed, a rush of pain, from somewhere deep on the left side of my body, yelled, what the fuck do you think you're doing? Don't do that! Get back on the slab-bed and lie perfectly still! Maybe take another round from humongous needle. I could taste a bitter bile, stale drug cocktail, rising in my throat.

I waited, holding on to the bed, trying not to reveal signs of distress.

"Take your time."

I straightened up, allowing my body adjustment time. I hadn't been fully upright since leaving the café. Back when standing was taken for granted. Before Horace and the motorcycle.

Bent at the knee, my left leg was slightly off the ground. This pleased the nurses, which delighted me.

"Pivot and lower yourself into the chair." Rescuers stood by, ready to grab me if I screwed up.

Not smooth, but a success. My bum landed in the wheelchair. *Which way to the exit?* Pivot transfer sounds trivial, but when you're banged up, it's like learning to run the 100-meter hurdles. Leg and arm movements must be precise. It's a wake-up call: stop taking routine movement for granted! From now on, you're a hurdler, nothing will be easy.

The doctor returned. He held a hospital clipboard, which was new. Out of a meeting with Finance and Administration? I didn't like the look. The clipboard made my guy look less like a TV doctor and more like the service advisor at the local dealership. "Bad news about your bike." They always look down at their clipboard, if it's bad news. You brought it in to have the secret software tweak thing done, but it's "bad news," and the proof is on the clipboard.

The doctor looked at the papers and back at me. Come on. Out with it, I wanted to say. You found nothing. Fit as a fiddle. Time to end the foofaraw. *Did they tell you, doc? I nailed pivot transfer.*

The doctor adjusted his glasses and looked down at the notes, to double check he wasn't handed the medical record for Testicular Cancer Patient #1, then said, "Most motorcycle accidents don't end well. Particularly not when Blue is involved."

So far, so good. Like service adviser saying, "Just had to turn that little impossible to reach adjuster screw with our very expensive secret tool."

"But." He was looking at the clipboard again. "Your ankle is badly broken. We'll schedule surgery. Time is critical."

I felt like he'd punched me in the gut. How can this be? They're going to slice me? Shouldn't I be bellowing like an Australian? Never having broken a body part, I had no basis for comparison. Sprained a finger once—hurt a hell of a lot more. *Maybe it's that horse needle? Maybe it hurts like hell and they've blocked the pain signals with their wonderful drugs?*

"Multiple shoulder fractures. Extensive soft tissue damage. We must run more tests. Possible surgery candidate."

Despite the drugs, Motorcycle Payback was making me nauseous. *I'll have to make the Bad News Update call.* The Road to Joy stops here, in a wheelchair.

He wasn't finished. More data on the clip board. "Multiple hip fractures. Severe bruising. Vital organs in that area. No obvious signs of organ damage or internal bleeding, but we'll need to monitor."

A bullet dodged.

"Can't rule out head or spinal injuries, given the extent of your impact injuries. CT and MRI scans will be necessary... as a precaution."

When you're in a stupor, bad news is still bad news, but it doesn't hit you over the head the way it should. It flares up and then sort of tickles you around the back of the head before sticking an uncomfortable finger in your ear.

"I'm afraid you've got a few months of recovery followed by a year of rehab in front of you. The orthopedic surgeon will see you tomorrow morning. We'll schedule surgery. We'll transfer you to regional."

He explained the risks and punch-lined the one-sided conversation with, "surgeries."

I don't know where it came from. It just slipped out. "I want to go home." It squeaked out in a weak, wee lad voice. *I want my mom! At least my bonus moms.*

The doctor explained there are, "Potentially serious medical complications" and repeated the word "peril" several times. He sounded like the risk lawyers I'd worked with. I know the routine. The lecture bounced off of me like water off a carnival duck's back. I was immune. Hardened. Didn't buy a word.

"Pretty sure I can make it home," I said calmly, trying to appear rational and execute a rapidly unfolding escape plan, based on sound logic: I have a good leg—my cousin gets around fine with one; what do I need my left arm and shoulder for? I'm right-handed! Get over the border into the arms of the government healthcare system I'd paid into for decades. Beats the hell out of going with the flow, away from home, going bankrupt. Rely on an unread *el cheapo* emergency travel insurance policy? I refuse to throw up my arms, roll the dice, and end up in a condemned, mouldy, rat-infested trailer! In the collision between healthcare and insurance companies, the patient always loses. Insurance giants make money by denying claims, not by paying out. That's the point of fine print and litigation departments. I'd heard lots of stories. I want to go home! To have peace of mind, not be bent by your wonderful drugs with Kathy Bates waiting eagerly at the regional hospital.

The doctor didn't look impressed. He had his, *I'm the expert here and I know what's best,* professional frown on his face. The nurses seemed shocked that leaving was even up for consideration. They were used to impact injury victims throwing in the towel. "There are significant medical risks." The doctor repeated and ran through several of them, as if I was another thick one, incapable of absorbing the message. "A complication would be serious. Time is not your friend. The sooner bones are set, the better the chance of success."

Yeah, and the sky could fall down or a box jellyfish could sting me in the rear end. I'd moved into competition mode. Can't be done? Just watch me!

Conrad was back and taking Ferry Memorial's

side. "Stay put. Do as you're told!"

Then he cheated and phoned his wife, an ex-operating room nurse. A genuinely impartial expert. Joanne put her foot down. "Don't leave the hospital! Are you nuts?" That advice rattled me. Maybe I am nuts? *She's an expert. Knows so much more than me. Maybe I should pay attention?*

Left brain chimed in: Joanne can't see the billing meter; she's used to a sheltered, socialized medical system. Doesn't know the horror of being a patient when government isn't picking up the tab. Doesn't realize that insurance lawyers are already scanning the el cheapo policy, arguing about which is the best loophole to clobber us with. Another damn risk-taking motorcyclist. We'll teach him to abuse the industry!

I faced a financial, not a medical decision. Forget Joanne's advice, both Left and Right agreed. Lean hard into the curve, accelerate out. Get the hell out of here. Don't become a patsy!

Scrape your pegs!

I hear words drifting around the room. "Blood clot. Trauma. Stroke. Bleeding. Bones not setting. Other injuries. Time is critical." I wasn't listening. All rhetoric; the song, Die Try'in was drowning the doctor out.

I was thinking, if I stay, I'll have to make the follow-up Hospital Call. "Well, I can't leave. They're planning to slice me. Better check with the real estate agent. See what the house is worth. And check to see if there are any mouldy rat-infested trailers for sale on the edge of town." Making the *I'm Out of the Hospital Call, but...* seemed a much better scenario.

As for Conrad, if you're in Emergency, with a person jettisoned off a motorcycle and busted up, what are you going to say? Sounds like a smart plan, buddy. Let's get you the hell out of here. Forget about listening to the medical experts. What do they know? You can drag your leg behind you, right? You know better, don't you, Jackass?

I convinced the doctor to give me a chance. Allow me to stand and demonstrate my one-legged mobility. I didn't mention the Lenny tips I'd picked up. *Not going to Mongolia, just across the border doc.* "After all, I'm not planning to walk home." Doctors, like motorcycle mechanics, aren't used to patients questioning their advice. I tried to be nice and appreciative.

I figured I could drive a rental with one good arm and leg. I was clever enough not to divulge that idea. Don't show your all your cards and never reveal escape plans! Haven't you watched Prison Break or Escape from Devil's Island?

◆ ◆ ◆

My left ankle was the size of a melon. The calf muscle had gone the opposite direction, shrivelled, and was in hiding. Parts of my leg were a disinfectant orange color. *Elephant Man, at least Elephant Man's left leg.* The sight of it was demoralizing. *Escape? Dragging this horrific thing with me.*

A nurse re-bandaged my lower leg. "Immobilization," they called it. A tall boot cast went on over the bandage. I was happy to have it out of sight. My left arm came out of the sling. I mustn't further damage my shoulder, the doctor warned. "Rest and ice, it as much as possible. To get inflammation under control."

When I was positioned for my attempt, an orderly provided a pair of tall crutches.

"Absolutely no weight on your left leg," the doctor instructed. He didn't need to; the slightest pressure triggered white-hot pain daggers and a foul bile stale taste that made me want to scream, puke, and pass out at the same time. A couple of warning blasts and everything I had at my disposal was focused on, "Absolutely no weight on my left side."

My leg couldn't move from the left hip, but the knee swung like a rusty hinge under my hospital dress, just enough to keep my cast boot off the floor as instructed. *See?* I looked proudly at the staff, like a four-year-old after their first two-wheel solo pedal. *Look, I can keep my leg off the floor, all by myself!*

Carefully, I placed a support stick under my left shoulder, as instructed by the doctor who had warned, "May not be possible." He was right. It produced white hot daggers. I was unable to put the slightest pressure on the crutch. Now what? The doctor didn't look surprised. He wore a told you so, not going anywhere, are you, expression?

Without a word, I switched the crutch to my right shoulder and attempted to hobble sideways rather than forward, keeping all weight off my left side, leaning to the right, alternating between the crutch and right leg. The orderly and nurse stood ready to intercede, should I start to topple over.

I started to topple. It sank in. I'm fucked up and I'm not Lenny. Carefully they lowered me back into the wheelchair. *Your goose is cooked.*

I can't imagine what wounded soldiers on a battlefield must feel. Especially ones drafted into a war they didn't feel was just. Forced participants in a farce. Shot to hell. All because political scientists refuse to outsource their responsibilities. No hope of survival unless the victims can rescue themselves. Drag their maimed Elephant Man bodies home. Or perish. In the mud. Without drugs. Lie and die, or start crawling.

"Ready to try again," I declared.

BULLHEADED

The task: move the body with available resources. An inch at a time. Forward and to the right. With extreme caution. Backward and left impossible, but are unnecessary movements in a pared down existence. Forward and right will get you where you need to go. An inch at a time. All concentration focused on the task at hand.

Up against my determination, the doctor had no option but to relent. Ferry Memorial is a hospital, not a prison. America, the land of the free, not North Korea or a risk management convention. I intended to assert my right to self determination. Scrape my pegs against the grain. Draw my fingernails down the chalkboard. Go home.

An administrator arrived with a release on a clipboard. Ten plus pages. Do you know pivot transfer, I wanted to ask? A test of medical knowledge. Admin vs Jackass Escapee. I smiled instead. Signed and initialled, acknowledging my decision was contrary to Ferry Memorial's advice. I committed to having surgery within three days. Three days, four days,

five days. Does it really matter? It's like manufacturers' maintenance intervals. They're designed for
the worst-case scenario, with a generous fudge factor
added on top of that. Tons of leeway. Same with
bone intervals, I'm sure. Well, not one hundred percent positive given I possess zero orthopedic knowledge and am a former medical fainter, but pretty sure
it might follow logic similar to vehicle maintenance
scheduling.

When I say, "acknowledged," remember, big
chunks of my mind were away on pain blocking as-
signment and not available for regular duties, like as-
sisting with rational thought. It's nonsensical of the
medical industry to pump patients full of drugs, then
ask them to read and understand a ten pager. Everyone, including Conrad, registered their disagreement
with my foolishness, but it is MY body and MY future on the line. I'm a motorcyclist. I do what I like!
Haven't you watched Rebel Without a Cause? As for
Conrad, he's ex-military. Everyone knows members
of the armed services swear an oath to no man left
behind.

I had a good supply of pain medication, multiple prescriptions, cold compress bags, a hospital
blanket, urine bottles, crutches (or in my case, a leaning stick and a spare leaning stick), a big hospital
pillow to, "keep my leg elevated," a DVD with X-rays,
a copy of the legal ten pager releasing Ferry Memorial from liability, a hospital gown, and a borrowed
wheelchair. I congratulated myself. *Where's that red*

blood line that leads to the exit?

At Ferry Memorial, they know how to comfort fallen bikers. Get them back on the road. To raise hell again one day. Follow Darkness Black next time down to the, "Welcome to Our Morgue" sign.

I sat in a borrowed wheelchair in my flimsy new dress. Once a proud mounted warrior. Now wounded and helmetless. A leg cast and bare toes replaced my giant boots. My uniform put away. A wanderer, now stuck at the hospital door, unable to leave. There is only one taxi in Republic, Washington, and it wasn't taking calls. I'd checked myself out of the hospital and stranded myself. Wheel out the door, then what?

◆ ◆ ◆

If you ride a motorcycle, think about being in a wheelchair. It may keep you out of one.

I sat in my wheelchair, arranging the hospital blanket to better cover my dress. Unable to progress, but totally unconcerned. I'm not too bullheaded to understand: when the vote is many to one, you're probably wrong. My mind worked, but like sludge. That's the way it is in Blobland. You're not the sharpest knife in the drawer. Trauma and drugs insist you plod along. All in good time. What's the rush? May have made a rookie mistake, but so what? Conrad will get it sorted.

I did nothing but wait, knowing Conrad would rectify the problem. He's good at that. Basically, that was my escape plan—Conrad will sort things out. *This is what he does, sort things out.* Even if I was firing on all cylinders, not visiting the outer limits, I'd have left it with Conrad. My solution would probably be no solution at all. "Let's pull my wheelchair with your GT. Only a mile to the motel." To make it sound sensible, I'd add, "Go easy on the gas!"

Conrad sorted it out.

BC nurse drove me in her personal car to the motel. Thank god for geographic bonding!

Conrad wheeled me into the motel handicap room. The chambermaid was leaving. She smiled, as if we shared a connection, both fucked up. Crystal meth, Skittles eating, chambermaid freak. I already missed the real angels of mercy. *Want to see my pivot transfer? Onto the bed.*

Conrad had a room a couple of doors down. It was well past dinner time; he'd scout for supper downtown, a block away. "Maybe soup or yogurt." No Skittles! I hadn't eaten a thing besides some cherries and one pastry, but, in Blobland, there is no appetite. I mentioned, "Soup or yogurt," so Conrad would feel better. A sense of normality. I was depending on him to sort things out and execute my escape.

"TV," Conrad asked?

I shook my head, no. I had drugs. Not cartoon watching drugs. Calm, dim light drugs.

Conrad left in search of food. I lay on the first of two queen beds. Flat on my back. Immobile. Boot cast, "not to be taken off." A lone wolf biker, now totally dependent. With a hospital urine bottle to relieve myself. Leg always elevated. Ice bag alternating between shoulder and hip. Scared that I had become another person. A less capable person. I might walk Pearl around the block one day, but never again around the lake? Grim reality sinks in when you're alone, in a dimly lit handicap room, thanks to a motorcycle. Doubting it was worth it. Where's the Road to Joy now?

When the lights went out, on night one of my escape, thank God for opioids.

GOING DOWN

Sometime after midnight, I went down. It wasn't the ghost of Horace the Horrible, it was my fucked up, Elephant Man body.

I'd woken under the hospital blanket, in my dress, flat on my back, leg still in the air, drugs on low, thinking, is this to be my future? Lie back. Do nothing? Blind acceptance? I popped more pills, but in the minutes before serenity arrived, Fear No Evil yelled at me, "Get your ass off this bed! Pee in the urine bottle if you must, then inch your way to the sink. Do what normal people do! Brush your teeth. Wash your face. Take control of your life! Don't be a disgrace! Are you going to lie on beds and wither away? Give up? Only twenty-five feet to the god damn sink. Get moving! How hard can it be? Or stay and become crystal meth, Skittles eating, decrepit, used-to-be-a-biker freak. Your choice.

I swung my right leg off the bed and onto the floor. Pushed myself up. Half a pivot. Even though I was in a handicap room, there wasn't enough space to maneuver the wheelchair without assistance. I inched forward between the beds and the wall, using a leaning stick and the bed as a safety net. It was frightening; I was on my own, in a strange dimly lit room, very unsteady, with a sink that was a marathon away. *How can you escape if you can't even make it to the bloody sink? Get on with it!*

I wanted to lie down, wait for the drugs to tell me, why bother? But reaching the sink was a test not to be denied. My future depended on teeth brushing. I made it as far as the second bed before my body started to shake like an out-of-control washing machine. I tried to regain balance with the doctor's words ringing in my ear, "Put weight on your left side and you'll be back in an ambulance." I twisted to help gravity and momentum take me down on my right side, in a space between the TV cabinet and the closet wall where Conrad had deposited my riding gear and other stuff. I dropped the leaning stick and crashed, terrified I wouldn't be getting back up on my own.

I lay on my right side, propped up by odds and ends, clenching my teeth. My phone, to be used to call Conrad if I needed anything, was on the bed table. I lay frozen at a thirty-degree angle, afraid of the damage report; *torpedoed again, captain. Bulkhead number four this time. Can't be sealed off. We're going down for sure!*

Go to Blobland. Let the drugs do their good work. It seemed like the best plan. *Forget about bulkhead number four! Skittle eating, crystal meth freak chambermaid will find you in the morning.*

Or Conrad? I didn't want him thinking, look at this guy. How pathetic is this? I'm going to sort this out by hauling his dumb ass back to Ferry Memorial. Damn the consequences! Let the nice nurses look after him. I'm ex-military, not a god damn nursemaid!

With all my weight on my right arm and leg, I slowly pushed and inched myself off the debris field until I was next to the second bed. It required everything I could muster, but eventually I managed to retreat to the safety of my bed. I can't explain the difficulty. Lie down on the floor. Get up using one side of your body only. For the full effect, take some tranquilizing drugs first. Every thirty seconds, allow an irate box jellyfish to sting your left side.

Sink mission aborted! Timidity and caution are essential lessons when you're fragile. No more damn the torpedoes. Decrepit Rule #1: Not Being Cautious May Kill You!

◆ ◆ ◆

When Conrad arrived on Monday morning to kickoff Day One operations, I was on the bed, in the compliant position. The clock was running.

"Coffee," he asked?

"Sure." I smiled. My coffee addiction remained intact.

"Good rest?"

"Great." *When will you have things sorted out?*

COULD HAVE
BEEN WORSE

Frontal collisions with stationary objects, like stags, cause the most severe motorcycle injuries. Lucky for me, we were ahead of schedule and Conrad had us on Slow Forward. My GT could have been going much faster when it met up with Horace. Would more speed have killed me? I survived relatively intact. If you have a motorcycle accident, are breathing, and don't look disfigured, you'll heard a lot of this:

"Could have been worse."

The question has occurred to me, did speed make me lucky or unlucky? Could it have been worse? If I had been travelling faster, even two miles an hour faster, Horace and I would not have met on the highway. A speck of time can make an enormous difference. Correct, Professor Hawking?

Meth freak chambermaid dropped in to change the towels. When she asked, "How you do'in?" she seemed to understand my, "Could have been worse," answer. Probably in the same boat as me. A slight alternation in time and she would have missed that first hit of drugs that trapped her.

❖ ❖ ❖

Conrad returned from the U-Haul dealership, twenty miles from town, with bad news; they did not have a truck up to the job of loading two bikes, driver, and one decrepit for a trip to Victoria. A stiff kick in the pants. Republic is a nice town, but not when it comes to rental transportation. No airport either. Our faith was in the hands of U-Haul and it was a bust.

I called Gigantic Insurance Company. "Can you help? It's an emergency medical situation. Exactly what my policy is all about. I need surgery within three days, but I'm stranded in a handicap motel room with a Skittles eating crystal meth freak chambermaid. I need your help! Who knows what will become of me on day four, if you don't do something?"

They took information, entered it in their supercomputer, and told me to, "Hold on." The computer came back with, "Released from Hospital." Made no difference that I had escaped in order to attempt to reach a hospital where the insurance company would be off the hook. They had me. Checking myself out gave my insurer a loophole, the one they choose to use against me. Section 9. Subsection 3. Clause 16. You get the picture: I was a victim of fine print. The fact that I was decrepit, required surgery, in pain, and was stranded and becoming increasingly demoralized, wasn't considered in the fine print. They only accepted hospital transfers, "bed-to-bed." It was a limitation of their *el cheapo* policy. I threatened to return to Ferry Memorial to readmit myself, but there was provision for that as well; once you're out, you're out. That's it—there's no going back. Let's add an unofficial rule:

Always Read the Fine Print! Or ride with a contract lawyer without an intercom.

Experience is something you get just after you needed it, the saying goes.

Now what? Here's a good thing to know about Conrad. He never said, "Told you so. Should have stayed put. You can be such a jackass." Didn't rub it in. If he says anything, it's with humor. Bob was like that. They'd have hit it off.

When all else fails, who bails you out? Family. I was lucky enough to have one. The family help desk doesn't have fine print. They'd already prepped a brother to drive me across the border. On the morning of Day Two, Ron arrived in Republic to fetch his little brother.

PART 7 –
MORORCYCLE-LESS

FALLING BROTHERS

We didn't grow up in a Secret Bunker. More like extras on the set of the Monty Python Lumberjack skit. With a little Huckleberry Finn and Nancy Drew thrown in.

Ron toyed with motorcycles until Rule #1 nailed him in Montevideo, Uruguay. Landed the third oldest sibling in a hospital for two months far from home. Not a stone's throw away, like me. Instead of a deer, a car bumped his Korean scooter. New medical challenges layered on top of older injuries, ones predicted to prevent him from living, then walking, let alone riding a motorbike in South America decades later.

My deer encounter, compared to Ron's experience, was summer vacation. When Ron picked me up, I didn't expect, "Thank God, you're safe, little brother! Everyone's worried sick. Wheel over here! Let me give you a hug." For Ron, it's a bump in the road, like being on the front line in Afghanistan, then witnessing a dust-up when you return home. Unless people are blown to smithereens, it doesn't register.

Not a big deal. Carry on. Gonna try for the free service dog?

"Not so bad," I assured big brother #2 as I demonstrated my pivot transfer prowess and sat in the Tracker. The Tracker Ron pulled behind his colossal RV, now staged an hour north, in Grand Forks, BC.

Ron left the borrowed wheelchair at the motel office, cutting me off from my mobility lifeline. *Can I hobble? Can I get to where I need to go, an inch at a time?* I didn't reveal signs of my distress. Ron was watching. *Mustn't be a crybaby, sobbing over the lose of a wheelchair.* If it were Barb or Joan, my bonus moms, the meetup would have been entirely different. But rather than a mom, the help desk sent the King of Bullheaded.

Skittle eating, crystal meth, chambermaid freak waved goodbye. I smiled and waved back. Surprisingly good customer service skills, I thought. For a meth freak. Maybe the tip I left by the TV helped? Probably a nice person, spit on by life. Dealing with her own Horace the Horrible. I hope she makes her escape and does well. I left a nice tip because it's admirable when people work at legitimate jobs to pay for their drugs, don't you think?

The Tracker backed out of its parking spot. "Escape in progress," I wanted to shout. Measured in feet not inches. *We're off! Ron, sound the horn! Drive by Ferry Memorial and honk again!*

No GT goodbyes. Abandoned behind a sign on a fence that said, "Trespassers will be shot! Survivors will be shot again!" As with TS-125, there was no option, I had to leave.

At eleven AM, we were on the highway. Clear blue sky and brilliant sunshine; a fine day for travelling. You expect, having gone through a traumatic event, the world, at least the weather, would be on side – gloomy. Reflective weather. But it was the exact opposite. Upbeat, does it get any better than this, kind of weather? Perfect for Conrad. He would be in the Cascades, riding through the mountain pass, gorgeous scenery, sweeping curves, aiming to catch the afternoon Washington State ferry home. He told me later that he was "nervous as hell," MRR cranked all the way up. Using traffic as a shield. Always scanning for deer. "Scheduling worked out well though. Right on time for the ferry." I missed him. And Bob.

I told Ron about my fall. I knew it was a pickup basketball game compared to the NBA final he'd starred in. Horrific to me, but benign to him. Like any respectable victim, I wanted to wallow in accident pity, but Ron isn't the guy. My accident was a day at the beach. I tried my best to make it sound like it could have been worse, because the reality is, Ron knows it can be a hell of a lot worse.

◆ ◆ ◆

In the nineteen sixties, when I was a youngster and Ron was barely twenty years old, he fell, well, not an actual fall. A crush. Not bashed by a road thanks to a deer, but pinned against a log by a yellowish, diesel fume belching, soulless Caterpillar. Where the hell was Buddha? Does he not ride in the circuitry of heavy equipment, Mr. Pirsig? You didn't mention in your stupid *Zen* book that the Big Man is selective. Two-wheel freedom machines only? No hitching rides on tracks, crawling through mud, with hard working loggers earning a living? No Zen and the Art of Heavy-Duty Mechanics? Is Buddha not comfortable submerged in grease?

Ron worked for Skeena Forest Products as a Whitewater Boom Man. He was little more than a Whitewater Boom Boy. The mighty Skeena is a large, fast-flowing river in north western British Columbia, home of cedar trees capable of living for a thousand years and growing up to 70m/230ft tall, unless a timber company knocked them down first, which is what Skeena River Forest Products was up to. The world had not yet done the math and figured out the sustainability equation. Tall, old growth cedars were valuable fair game.

Ron was the youngest on a crew of a dozen men, half of whom lived in a small logging camp nearby. The others, like Ron, commuted in a bus from town. My brother was born strong, athletic, stubborn, hard playing and hard working. He was made to be a Whitewater Boom Man. Riding a motorcycle is child's play compared to riding a log down the Skeena river. He loved it. *Paid to ride a log down a river? Are you kidding me?* The mere suggestion of such an occupation today would horrify regulators. I'm obstinate, but may have to side with the *we're-here-to-protect-you* crowd on this one.

Ron led a small crew of older men that constructed booms, logs chained together in a backwater, to form a log corral. Timber, dumped into the Skeena upstream, would float down the river to be herded into a waiting trap. Three hundred logs to fill one boom. A river tug helped direct the careening wooden missiles toward the opening. Along the river bank and in the backwater, Ron jumped from log to log with his peevee pole, a tool used to hook and move logs, to push timber away from shore, break up jams, and direct the fallen trees into the boom. Like herding cattle into a chute, except on a dangerous, fast-flowing, large river. Once a boom was full, a tug would shepherd it toward a pulp mill and lumber mills forty miles away, at the edge of the Pacific Ocean.

Whitewater Boom Men

Ron loved the work. It was easy and natural for him. No fear. Not daunting, as it would be for a reasonably cautious person. Not the hell of an office, or university campus, or the inside of a store. Had he been born in Wyoming; my brother would have been a cowboy. Enjoyed the Cowboy Breakfast at Rock Creek. Hung out with other cowpokes. Beat the shit out of anyone who needed a whoop'in. Rode a horse and stayed the hell away from heavy equipment and motorcycles.

Building booms requires skill, muscle, balance, and on-the-fly engineering. There are different building techniques depending on the time of year and the water level. The boom sticks that makeup the corral are secured together with chains. The ends of the logs that will form the opening, rest on shore, tethered by cables, to secure the boom, until it's time to position it in the river. Today's few remaining Whitewater Boom Men are Whitewater Boom Persons, heavily clad in safety gear and regulation. They follow the Ten Rules of Booming, unlike in Ron's day when it was, *Just About Anything Goes.*

Boom Building

A big powerful bulldozer pulled the boom stick joints tight at the build site. The boom crew would lash the logs together with chains and then call the dozer to hook on and pull the boom into place. At 2:20 on a sunny summer afternoon, Ron waved the Cat over. He jumped off a log to take the winch cable as he had done a hundred times before. His body was between a log and the Cat in a tight space. WTF? Risk Mitigation Guy, where are you? My brother needs you! Stop writing up, Do Not Use This Power Tool While Bathing, and go where you're needed! I wish. It was early days. Skeena River Forest Products was in the lumber business, not the protect our young gung-ho workers business. It seems to be true; *there is no middle ground.*

This time the bulldozer didn't stay put and wait for the command to move forward, to draw the boom sticks tight. The driver, in a daze from the long hot summer work days, reversed. By the time Ron realized what was about to happen, he was trapped (he admits to day dreaming about his girl friend at the time). He screamed at the driver, but the Cat kept crawling back. He may have roared, "I don't want to die. Especially not like this! My girl friend is waiting for me." I don't know? Ron only remembers feeling his bones breaking. My antler nightmares don't compare to bones-crushing-your-body-toward-death. You see why I told my brother, "Could have been worse?"

A boom man threw his axe at the Cat. It clanked against metal, knocking the driver out of his stupor. The machine stopped inches from certain death-by-heavy-machinery. In unfathomable pain, with internal bleeding, and unable to see, Ron lay on the ground surrounded by five loggers who had no idea what to do. *We're loggers in shock, not EMTs or battlefield doctors.* I was lucky; I had the best of the best, direct descendants of Zadkiel. Not sweaty shocked loggers with cork boots, chain saws, axes, and peevee poles.

The Cat crushed Ron's spine, hip, and pelvis. He was in tremendous pain when the loggers loaded him into a river boat. He was flown from Terrace, with a doctor who didn't expect him to make it, to Vancouver. A police motorcycle escorted his ambulance to Vancouver General Hospital. Maybe the motorcycle was a good omen? Buddha onboard? He stayed at VGH for two months, before being transferred to a rehabilitation center. When we were in the Tracker, I didn't mention my nightmarish sink calamity. Or how wonderful today's drugs are. Mostly we chatted about the countryside; Ron had not visited the area prior to my escape.

Ron would never walk again, the doctors said. Seems like a safe prediction for a patient crushed by heavy equipment. But he did. No running or whirling dervish dancing, but he manages, unassisted. Only possible if you're the King of Bullheaded. Ron worked, raised three sons and a daughter, renovated houses, got divorced, travelled, sucked in plenty of pain, saw many doctors, and eventually hopped on a scooter in Montevideo where Deadeye Dick nailed him. How unfair is that? Death Lottery fell short, so let's see how this bastard handles the Motorcycle Draw? "Damn," DD must shake his head. "Those brothers are too stubborn. Next time I'll have Radical finish them with his knife."

I was too young to fathom what had happened to my indestructible big brother at the time of the accident. I grew up with a *don't mess with me, bucko* attitude. *Tangle with kid brother and you'll be up against mighty defenders. You sure as hell don't want that!* I couldn't comprehend, one had gone down. *And, if my sisters have to get involved, you're in for one hell of an articulate lecture on appropriate behaviour and proper etiquette!*

As we rode north in the Tracker, Ron's story played in my mind. It kicked me in the cerebellum, sending shivers down my spine. Are you really going to whine about your little deer incident for the next

year or two? Like Screamer going on about his nip?
End up like Lenny?

Scrape your pegs, you sniffling little boy! Decrepit Rule #2: Be Stubborn in a Good Way.

◆ ◆ ◆

Early afternoon we pulled to a stop beside
the big RV. Ron, the mobility expert, had a fix
for my pathetic hobbling non-performance. "Forget the leaning sticks. Next to useless." Tucked
away in a secret storage compartment were a pair of
elbow crutches. Instead of being positioned under
the shoulder, a cuff goes around the forearm and the
hands latch on to horizontal grips. Elbow crutches
distribute weight in the arms, relieving the shoulder.

Movement was still a struggle, but now I could
confidently manage two inches at a time. I wonder why the medical experts never suggested elbow
crutches? Part of their scheme to thwart my escape?
Or was it a case of experience trumps medical col-
lege?

In front of the RV entrance were three foldable
metal steps. No handrail. It may as well have been
the Great Wall of China—an impossible barrier. An

early lesson in mobility friendly construction. Back in the Tracker, we drove to the community hospital, more a first aid and logistics center than a full-service hospital. My brother Lance, a year and a half older than me and a former member of the Royal Canadian Mounted Police, had called to give them an order: "Injured motorcyclist incoming. Escapee from the US billing system. Be prepared!" *If there's any trouble, I'll mount my horse and be there in a week!* Actually, Lance never rode horses or motorcycles, but he did fall over a waterfall.

◆ ◆ ◆

Lance fell. Really fell. Not Crushed. FELL in order to be CRUSHED. Into a fast-flowing stream and then head first down a three hundred foot / ninety-two-meter waterfall, like plunging off the top of Big Ben in London. He was thinking, no heavy equipment in this forest, what could possibly go wrong? It was a beautiful day, like the day I met up with Horace. I had an appointment with a motel room. Lance had an appointment with a dot on a map.

He was an eighteen-year-old boy, working a summer job timber cruising in the Nass Valley, the process of mapping an area and measuring the vol-

ume and quality of standing and downed timber before it is harvested. It's now part of an indigenous
tourist area. Some of the most beautiful scenery to be
seen without travelling to the cosmos. It's the heredi-
tary home of the Nisga'a people. There's a lava field
and a terrific motorcycle road—Conrad and I made
the trek to Terrace to check the Nisga'a Highway out,
year one before Horace. And visit one of my bonus
moms and painter, Joan and her family. On the drive,
I had plenty of time to think about how one can be
an artist and still be perfectly balanced, like Leonardo da Vinci. Joan and Leonardo could ride together.
Horses or motorcycles. Then a Moment of Absolute
Clarity: of course, they could paint motorcycles on
ceilings, like Michelangelo did on the Sistine Chapel.
Pay homage to the Moses dirt bike! And touch-up
Leo's Mona Lisa by adding a motorcycle.

Years earlier, Lance and his twenty-year-old
work mate, Rick, climbed out of a helicopter on an
August morning, in a remote forest in north western British Columbia. Young explorers. Dropped into
the wilderness to join bears, mosquitoes, moose and
whatever nature had in store for them. No communication systems. No GPS. They were old school
explorers tramping through land man had never
seen before. No forestry company mandatory safety
compliance training. Mary, the receptionist at head
office, was in charge of risk awareness. She updated
the Safety Sign that said, XX days since the last accident. Unless there was a recent accident, in which

case the rule was, wait a couple of weeks before up-dating the sign. Back in the day, you were on your own. Government was your little sister, not your big brother. As I said, there is no middle ground.

The boy's objective: find a reasonable route to a predetermined dot on a topographical map. Plot the path on paper. Here's a compass and a chain to measure distance. Twelve miles to the dot. Better get a move on! In a later step, others would use their map, retrace their route to reach the dot and inspect the value of the old-growth trees that stood waiting, their days numbered. An environmental conscience would soon weigh-in on the forested lands, but on that summer day, the timber was fair game. Lumber and pulp mills have ravenous appetites.

Lance led, operating the compass. Rick fol-lowed, holding the far end of the measuring chain. Each compass reading translated into a visual land-mark, usually a prominent tree, used to guide the pair, in incremental steps, toward the dot on the map. Off they went, fixated on one landmark after another, never knowing what lay in their path until they covered the ground. At times, nature forced them to deviate off course, go around an impossible barrier, before locking back on, taking a shot directly at the dot, always making a commotion to warn wildlife— stay the hell away from us! That was the only safety tip—make lots of noise, if you don't want to become bear food.

On this August day, the boys encountered a fast-flowing stream in a shallow ravine. It stood between them and the next landmark, a tree that Lance kept fixed in his line of sight, their immediate objective. My brother stood, his heavy logging boots on rocks above the edge of the creek. I can jump back, he thought, away from the water. *After all, I was on the high school volleyball team. I know about jumping and keeping my eye on the ball. I can jump back, not lose sight of the big crooked tree, our direction marker. Our guide to the dot.*

A boot slipped. Then he was sliding toward the water. Hands on the compass. His attention still welded on the landmark. The thought of jumping backward dismissed. *Maybe a wet foot? Not so bad.* He eyed the opposite shore, but the rocks there were too steep and jagged to attempt a crossing. *A wet foot it is.*

Fast-flowing mountain water is deceptive. Streams look peaceful, flowing through undisturbed nature, but carry the massive power of an unstoppable force. Sir Isaac could calculate the energy, but just imagine being hit with fifty fire hoses. A boot slipped into the stream. And then the other. There was no hope. The current was far too strong, and heavy gear weighted the boy down. The waterfall waited, a few car lengths down stream, its proximity determined by the route to the dot. A three-hundred-foot / ninety-two-meter plunge to certain death. *You boys should be home, fooling around, not out here, tramping through my forest. Bag groceries if you must have a*

*summer job! Or serve soft ice cream. What do you think
you're doing here, on your own, eyeing my trees?* The
current picked my brother up and flung him over the
cliff. *Off with you! Be gone!* No Buddha. He was busy
hanging out in Mr. Pirsig's old Honda at that time.

Years later, I fell out of a canoe and almost
drowned in my own fast-flowing water. Had fate not
rescued me, I would have enjoyed a peaceful, tranquil,
willing end of life. What awaited Lance was the exact
opposite, a horrific bombardment against rocky out-
croppings before bleeding to death, as water held him
under at the bottom of the falls.

His six-foot body dropped over the edge. He
nosedived toward his end of days. Faced with the
shock and terror of what was about to happen, most
people would black out, retreat into a protective
daze in order to shield their mind from the insanity
of what lay ahead, their brain matter hopelessly confused by the incomprehensible situation. Life does
not prepare you for plummeting down a waterfall or
falling from the top of Big Ben.

Lance knew he was not going to survive if his
body shot into whatever waited at the bottom of
the falls. What to do? "Time kind of stood still.
Life does flash before your eyes." Valley of Death, I
thought, listening to my brother talk? He was definitely headed in that direction. "Memories," was the
word he used. "They prompted me to want to save
myself." Physically close to death, but mentally,

Lance never conceded, as I had when I was trapped in my death stream. I got a video. Lance got memories. Eerily similar. But maybe different? One a call to action. The other an acceptance. Each of us pushed by water toward our Valley of Death. Ron was beside the Skeena river. Death by water. Like Bob. What happened to Bob?

"You know how, when you're a kid, you think you can jump, just before you hit the ground to save yourself? It was sort of like that. I thought I could jump before I hit the bottom to save myself. More manoeuvre than jump, but the same idea. I can save myself, I thought. I know it sounds silly, but I really did believe I would figure something out." Hopelessness and despair would have seized me, I'm sure. *I'm going to die and I'm just a kid. Mother of God, why me?* But Lance wasn't overcome. "I had time to think. It was surreal. As if it were happening in slow motion." The opposite of my collision on Highway 20, where there was no time to react. Tumbling down a tall waterfall, if you have presence of mind, gives you time to think: *What can I do to prevent my imminent death?* Talk about a Newtonian moment! Exactly what can you do if you find yourself plummeting down a waterfall?

Scape Your Pegs!

Lance glimpsed a rock ledge poking through the cascading water below him. He had dropped about 150' / 46m with at least another 100' / 30m to go. Somehow, he swung his body enough to aim his big lumberjack "cork" boots at the ridge. His boots hit the outcropping, slowing his momentum. He spotted a second lower ledge to his right. One without sharp jagged edges, just out of reach. He forced his body to roll, moving it against the power of the water that wanted only to force him down. His body moved far enough right to hit the second rock ledge. Slammed into its surface. Rock rather than asphalt. Head against stone, like me, but without protection, aside from desperately flapping arms. The force of the water pushed Lance against the ledge until it marooned him, snagged on a rock, dangling beside a waterfall. Sounds awful, but he was extremely lucky.

Somehow the hatchet he carried, strapped to his belt, had ripped his hip open. He could feel the blade gnawing away at flesh.

Briefly overwhelmed, he lost consciousness. Eyes could not see; skin from his scalp slapped over them. Blood drained from his forehead over his face, painting the falling water, forming a red line to death at the bottom. There would be 97 stitches above his eyebrows, across his scalp to close the wound. Still, his mind persisted. He remembers coming to and counting to remain conscious. To hold on. Hold on to life. Determined that his fate would not be — bled to death, alone, without his girl friend or mom and dad, or little brother, beside a waterfall in the middle of nowhere. He could wiggle Toes and Fingers. Young and strong, being paralyzed would have been worse than death.

No angels of mercy, anywhere close by. Just Rick, up above. Blinded by skin and blood, Lance could hear Rick screaming. Hollering in terror. Bleeding and drained of strength, there was no communicating over the roar of the water. Rick had to desert his wounded buddy. He raced through the bush toward a logging road.

Lance waited. Counting. Trying to push skin against bone to slow the bleeding.

When Rick reached the road, again luck was there—it delivered a radio equipped logging truck within minutes. Back on the rock ledge, Lance silently counted. *Perhaps my last seconds?* There is no being impatient. I waited on a highway. Lance waited on a cliff beside water. What can you do? Wait.

A crew of loggers with a stretcher rescued the young student. Carried him out to a waiting helicopter which flew to Mills Memorial Hospital in Terrace. Lance couldn't see through the blood and bandage wrapped around his head. Anyway, it wasn't his first helicopter ride.

By coincidence, a national TV crew was in Terrace doing a story. They diverted to Mills Memorial for the much better, Miracle Boy Survives Waterfall, story. Miracle Boy made the national newscast and other news groups picked up his story. Lance got his minute of fame the hardest way possible. Unfortunately, no talking; his voice box, bruised from the fall, the Prince of Bullheaded was speechless for weeks.

It was a miracle. Not a single broken bone. No internal bleeding. Maybe Buddha was there? Hidden in the compass? My brother looked like he'd been to hell and back though. I was sixteen years old when I reluctantly set foot inside Mills Memorial with my parents. As an active, physically strong lad, I had a severe case of anti-blood medical neurosis that would instantly drain me, and put me on the verge of passing out. My kryptonite. I barely made it to my brother's room standing. I took a quick look. Saw his head was all bandage. Tubes ran into his body. Horrific! I was a second away from passing out. It's no way to show support; I fled or rather dragged myself down the yellow line. Escape or be laid low. Stare down at the line on the floor that leads to fresh air. Another minute and the angels of mercy would have been attending to me instead of Miracle Boy. How wrong would that be? Of course, that was before I became a tough outlaw biker.

They released Lance from the hospital in less than a week. He went on to do great things. With his wife Sharon and their two children. Skipped the Niagara Falls honeymoon when he got married.

At Grand Forks Hospital, they took more X rays, consulted with other hospitals and agreed the best option for me was to be close to home, in a full-service hospital. On Wednesday, August 21, with assistance, I flew to Victoria and, at five o'clock on Day Three, was wheeled into Royal Jubilee, a five hundred bed state of the art hospital half an hour from home. An orthopedic surgeon operated the next morning, Day Four, technically breaking the terms of my agreement with Ferry Memorial by a day. The hospital got to work pronto, repairing my impact injuries. They were very concerned about bone timing calculations, just like Ferry Memorial. I guess bones do have a narrower time tolerance than vehicle service tasks.

◆ ◆ ◆

My oldest brother, Dave, began the Falling Brothers tradition. He swung out on a homemade trapeze, across the face of a rock bluff, lost his grip, fell and bounced off the ground below. How con-

ventional. Right? Probably laughed when he hit
—Dave doesn't practice Curmudgeonly Jackass-ism—
he's a jokester. I suppose we were brothers in need of
tanks. Luckily, we have two sisters, or for me, two
bonus moms, Barb and Joan, to pull us up and out of
whatever swamp we find ourselves in. Plus, Anita
(Dave's wife) and Sharon. Joan never joined the Royal
Canadian Mounted Police, but is a horse rider. Horses
have more sense than motorcycles and know not to
run into deer. My niece has a bike, and Joan's grandson
recently purchased his first motorcycle. Uh Oh!

Relatives should not ride motorcycles!
Stumpy is proof of that. If you're a relative, listen to
Risk Management Guy. But a tank! Two Motorcycle
Decrepits per family only!

My second mom, Barb, scares me when she
drives a car. If she buys a motorcycle, the brothers
will conduct an intervention. Lenny will come and
wiggle his stump like a warning finger. Do not buy
that scooter! He lives in Vancouver close to Barb and
Aunt Minnie.

❖ ❖ ❖

I was the last brother to end up in hospital,
banged up. For two weeks, I recovered in Royal Ju-

bilee, learning how to cope without the use of half of my body, the Elephant Man half. My roommate was another bike accident victim. He'd hit a curb on his bicycle, toppled over, and broke his hip. I guess there's a Bicycle Lottery as well.

My family, Dori, Colin, and Monica kept me company. Monica works as an RN at Royal Jubilee, so it was more like I dropped by to visit her. Lenny came over from Vancouver. No spider plant. Bob brought Kirkland Almonds.

It would have been great if Bunny, my cat, could have stayed to help with my recovery. I didn't ask; assumed they would consider it a little whacko and out of character for a biker outlaw dude. After a week, I was able to wheel outside to the courtyard to see my dog, Pearl. Pearl's much better at over-the-top emotional displays than Bunny, but not as deep a thinker. Bunny's great at staring blankly at nothing, just like I was on my drugs.

When you're in a hospital, motorcycle-less, and Bunny-less, you can't help but think, why me? I know the answer: MOTORCYCLES.

AFTER THE FALL

There is a gradual progression from motorcycle to hospital bed, to wheelchair, to motorized mobility scooter, to crutches, to walker, to water walking, to cane, to trekking poles, to walking slowly, building strength and learning what your limitations are likely to be. This my friends, is Motorcycle Payback. Remember Newton? Every force has an equal and opposite reaction? JOY has a price: MOTORCYCLE PAYBACK.

The best advice I received from doctors and therapists is worth repeating: people who have a positive attitude and work at recovering do well. People who become resigned, feel sorry for themselves and do little, quickly go downhill.

Another way of putting it—if you tell yourself, Good enough. Fuck it! You'll end up a blob. If you're stubborn, you're in the game. I didn't share family perseverance stories with my doctors and therapists. I could have said, "Listen to this," but I felt it might make my repair experts less enthralled with my progress. *Oh. You had examples? It's in your genes? That's much less impressive than recovering all on your own.*

My wife, Dori, looks after me while I do minuscule exercises in my room in the basement, the staircase barring the way to the main floor for now. I point my busted foot toward imaginary hour marks on a clock and shrug my busted shoulder. When actions that trivial become your Mount Everest, you know it'll be a long slow climb to the summit. If you're stubborn, you repeat twice as often as instructed by your in-home therapist.

ZEN AND THE ART OF MOTORCYCLE RIDING

T wo months after my release from Royal Jubilee, Bob flew into the Thompson River. I'd been thinking about my falling brothers and how they handled their experiences. To add to that, now there was the question of what happened to Bob? As I recuperated and researched, the puzzle pieces formed a picture.

I believe Bob had it figured out. There was more to my motorcycle friend than met the eye, but I had never been able to put my finger on what it was. Now, on reflection, it seems obvious. When I joked about Buddha hitchhiking on his Multistrada, Bob explained, "It's conceptual. When you ride, you're connected."

"So?"

"Enlightenment is the interconnectedness of all things."

"So?"

He joked about being a Transformer. The shift that happens *Before-Motorcycle* and *On-Motorcycle*. The constant swing between nothingness and awareness that can happen when you're riding. How the drone of the engine and the wind can make your mind think about nothing and then everything. Days and months of life happen in minutes and hours on a motorcycle. Riding is a quest, like life condensed in time. The perfect ride doesn't last long, life is like that. It changes. Always forward to the next event.

In our minds, Bob and I were hardened survivors. Curmudgeonly Jackasses. But we had the terminology wrong; "curmudgeon" and "Zen" can't co-exist. Like my falling brothers, clearly Bob processed a touch of Zen, the ability to deal with consequences. I just hadn't watched the right YouTube videos to put an appropriate label on it.

I've said the Motorcycle Riding Rules are about **Ability** and **Awareness.** But it should be **Ability, Awareness, and Accountability.** The world is what it is, the rider must be accountable. Bob knew that. "You are in charge of your ride. Not Buddha." It is Zen and the Art of Motorcycle Riding. Try maintenance if you want to take a philosophical cosmic journey with Robert, rather than ride the Road to JOY.

Life hands you experience. Some of it makes sense. Other parts make you wonder? Why was Horace on Highway 20? Why did a bulldozer crush the King of Bullheaded? Push Lance over a waterfall and

Dave off inanimate objects? Karma? The law of cause and consequence? When you ride, you can't stop the rain that pelts you for hours and eventually seeps into your skin no matter what you wear. Or the sun and heat that fry you like a battered pickle. But you can be skillful about the way you react.

Life handed my brothers horrible accidents. Who knows why? Let's not speculate on controlling cause. Each brother responded with a deep determination. They were skillful and accountable, taking responsibility for outcomes. Zen? Karma? Buddhist-like?

As a consequence of Thinking, and with guidance from YouTube, I'm adding "Zen" to the way I define my life practice now. Sure, I'm a jackass and possibly a curmudgeon, but I am one who will consciously be accountable for consequences. Instead of cursing and Why Me's? it'll be What Next? The extent of my recovery and how I manage with what I become, is up to me. Think of yourself as a Zen Jackass, and the consequences will be better than being a Curmudgeonly Jackass, don't you agree? One paltry word. I feel better about myself already. Rebranded. The new and improved me!

I suspect Bob had the great ride of causality figured out. He never blamed, he dealt with consequences. If I suggested swapping "Curmudgeon" for "Zen." "Just a word," he'd say. I think. Probably, that's what he'd say. I wish to god he were here now to talk it through. To assure me, "Yes, I knew all along. It has nothing to do with maintenance. Nothing what so ever."

Bob owned two motorcycles; both were his sanctuaries. He rode the cruiser to his end. Or his next beginning? Reincarnated or? ... They say he had pancreatic cancer. Who knows why? My motorcycle friend dealt with his fatal disease. He scraped his pegs.

RIDE AGAIN?

It's been months since Horace and I met up. The scene replays in my mind, sometimes in a nightmarish way. Other times, as a question, "What's next?" People ask, "Will you ride again?" If you can.

"Probably not," I answer when asked. It'd be crazy, right? My number would go back in the draw. Family members would ask, "Didn't you learn anything? One Hospital Call is enough!"

I have nothing but time on my hands. "Will I climb back on," is a question that eats up a lot of it? Bones mend. Memories diminish. Soft tissue pain dulls. In a year, I may be physically capable, but will I be comfortable, in body and mind, on a motorcycle?

I admit to being fearful. Not so bullheaded. I read stories about riders who "got right back on the next week." "I climbed on with my cast." "Don't be a weenie! Get the fuck back on!" These are real bikers. True outlaws! Me, I'm a Zen Jackass or, as Marta says, "A jackass whose number came up." She's requested I transfer funds from the motorcycle travel budget to

Snacks and Washroom Maintenance. Maybe. I enjoy the battered pickles more now that I can't ride to Wyoming for the Cowboy Breakfast.

I spend hours lying on my back browsing. "Maybe I'll find a Recovery Bike," I tell Bunny. "One that fits my circumstances? Immune to Kamikaze deer. More therapeutic tool than motorcycle." After many years, I miss not having a motorcycle resting in the garage. To talk things over with. The house seems empty without one. You'd think I'd hate motorcycles, but I don't. Bunny understands. There is more than one way to skin a cat...

Recovery is a tough slog. There are times you want to throw up your hands and be done with it. No! Be stubborn in a good way, god dammit! Be accountable. At a minimum, healing must get me to where climbing on is my decision. I work at recovering, it's my job now that I'm a Zen Jackass.

Mostly, I don't want to concede to Marta. "I guess we could move all of your Travel Budget into Snacks and Washroom Maintenance. Won't be going far on that mobility scooter. Plus, you've been eating an awful lot of battered pickles."

A PANDEMIC

It's been seven months since my number came up. Now there's a pandemic called COVID-19 scaring the shit out of people, including my rehabilitation services. Gone are my massages, needling, sonic vibrators, physiotherapies, steam room, sauna, kinesiology, water walking, and exercise room. Thanks a lot, pandemic! All my get-better-ammunition taken away. Life handed the world and my recovery a challenge. The good news is, I'm sticking with Zen Jackass-ism. I refuse to say, Good enough. Fuck it! Done in by a pandemic.

No, I'm carrying on, on my own, in my own way.

Thanks to COVID-19, Marta is making her own pickles. She calls them: The World's Battered and in a Pickle, Pickles. I'm sure Risk Management would like to slap some warning labels on them.

Kickstands Up, my friends.

I'll report back on my next stop, in More Scraping Pegs! Thanks for riding with me.

Visit our site for more information:

https://beatenstickpress.wixsite.com/mysite

APPENDIX

APPENDIX A – RULES

<u>Ten Motorcycle Riding Rules</u>:

#1. Everyone is trying to kill you!

#2. Don't Kill Yourself by Doing Something Stupid!

#3. Ignoring Motorcycle Physics May Kill You.

#4. Your Motorcycle May Be Trying to Kill You!

#5. Complacency Can Kill You.

#6. Your Own Noggin is Trying to Save You.

#7. Be Stubborn in A Good Way.

#8. Your Number May Come Up.

#9. Irritants May Get Your Goat.

#10. The Multiplier Effect is Also Trying to Kill You!

If you're tailoring or adapting the rules, be careful not to confuse Rule and Guideline. Rules are "explicit." Ignore a rule and there will be consequences. Guidelines are "suggestions." Take it or leave it. "Don't worry. Just a guideline." Like don't eat butter, eat margarine instead. Look how that turned out. They don't really know, so it's a guideline. Do what ever the hell you want. Taking the Motorcycle Riding Rules as guidelines may kill you, so don't do that.

I suppose Professor Hawking chose not to include rules in a *Brief History of Time* because they'd be guidelines no matter what he called them. He didn't want to cast suspicion on his academic work. Ditto for the *Zen* book. Let's face it, until motorcycle engineers are able to verify what's going on in the cosmos, it's speculation. We don't need another astrology rule like, each day chariots pull the sun across the sky. That's not even a guideline, it's pie-in-the-sky.

Nine Guidelines for Making Brussels Sprouts Tolerable or Seven? Doesn't have to be ten because people know it's culinary suicide. No matter what the number, it has no validity. Rule Validity is important. If you're creating guidelines, go crazy. Fill your boots.

Conrad and I added, *leave early stop early,* but it is not a Rule. *Leave early stop early* doesn't have enough substance to stand with the ten. Is leaving ten minutes late going to kill you? No, because it's just something a couple of jackasses made up. It's not a rule. Maybe a weak guideline?

Ten is always the correct number for a list, according to Marketing. That's why there are so many top ten lists and the ten rules of important things. If there are eleven important things, Marketing will insist two rules be rolled into one so the count remains at ten. Apparently, consumers will not purchase a product that comes with nine or eleven rules. "Hope Rule #11 doesn't sink us," Marta says referring to the additional Rule to be introduced in *More Scraping Pegs*.

APPENDIX B – VALVES

Valve Adjustment:

1. Go to YouTube
2. Search for your bike's How-to Adjust Valves videos.
3. Turn YouTube off.
4. If your bike has a valve adjustment symptom like pre-ignition or over heating, go to #6.
5. If your bike has no symptoms and is running fine, get a second opinion from Buddha before blowing your money.
6. Take your bike and your credit card to Service.

AFTERWORD

If you enjoyed Scraping Pegs, please consider leaving a review. Reviews help authors and, in this book's case, help spread the word about the JOY of motorcycling and the need to be skillful and aware.

ACKNOWLEDGEMENT

Editor: Mark Gint, for showing the way.

Proof: Joan Brady, grammar savant

Readers: Dennis Kent, Barb Stewart, Conrad Moller

My Angels of Mercy:
- Republic, Washington Emergency Services and the Good Samaritans of Highway 20.
- Ferry Memorial and Royal Jubilee Hospital staff.
- The Stewart Family Help Desk.

The Copley Park Dog Moms: Donna Ramsden Kent, Emily MacDonald, Lye Fong, Colleen Sullivan, Karen Galway, Katie Rowat, Telay Telay, Jes Sugrue

Help In Many Ways: Conrad Moller. Dori, Colin, & Monica.

ABOUT

Scraping Pegs, The Truth About Motorcycles (Book 1)

January 2021

The Joy of Motorcycles, More Scraping Pegs (Book 2)

Fall 2021

Do the worst rides make the best stories? Is the worst ride better than not riding?

Scraping Pegs is a bold narrative exploring two of the fundamental questions of life: why ride and how not to die.

Printed in Great Britain
by Amazon

59669591R00166